Ghosts of London: Ten Haunted Places in The City

Edward Turner

Published by Oliver Lancaster, 2023.

While every precaution has been taken in the preparation of this book, the publisher assumes no responsibility for errors or omissions, or for damages resulting from the use of the information contained herein.

GHOSTS OF LONDON: TEN HAUNTED PLACES IN THE CITY

First edition. July 8, 2023.

Copyright © 2023 Edward Turner.

ISBN: 979-8223773757

Written by Edward Turner.

Also by Edward Turner

Ghosts of Paris: Ten Haunted Places in the City of Love
Ghosts of London: Ten Haunted Places in The City

Ghosts of London: Ten haunted places in The City

EDWARD TURNER

Introduction

GHOSTS OF LONDON: TEN HAUNTED PLACES IN THE CITY

The history of the Viaduct Tavern

The most famous ghostly sightings

Theories about the nature of the hauntings

Personal accounts of ghostly experiences

Chapter 5: The Grenadier Pub

History of the Grenadier Pub

The most famous ghostly sightings

Theories about the nature of the hauntings

Personal accounts of ghostly experiences

Chapter 6: The Bank of England

Historical background of the Bank of England

The most famous ghostly sightings

Theories about the ghosts' origins and motivations

Personal accounts of ghostly experiences

Chapter 7: The Theatre Royal, Drury Lane

The history of the Theatre Royal, Drury Lane

The most famous ghostly sightings

Theories about the ghosts' origins and motivations

GHOSTS OF LONDON: TEN HAUNTED PLACES IN THE CITY

Introduction

London's haunted history

London's haunted history is a fascinating topic that has captured the imaginations of people for generations. From the Tower of London to the old haunted pubs, the city is steeped in legend, myth, and mystery.

The Tower of London is one of the most famous haunted locations in London. This historic fortress has been the site of many executions and murders, and it's said to be haunted by the ghosts of those who died there. The White Lady and the headless ghost are among the most well-known apparitions that are said to haunt the Tower.

Highgate Cemetery is another famous haunted location in London. It's said to be home to the infamous "Highgate Vampire," a creature that was allegedly sighted in the 1970s. There have also been numerous reports of ghostly apparitions and strange noises coming from the cemetery.

The London Dungeon is a popular attraction that's known for its gruesome displays and interactive exhibits. But it's also said to be haunted by the spirits of those who suffered in the dungeons. Visitors have reported feeling a chill in the air or seeing apparitions while inside.

The Viaduct Tavern and Grenadier Pub are both old pubs that are said to be haunted by ghostly patrons. The Bank of England is said to be haunted by a ghostly figure known as the "Black Nun," while the Theatre Royal, Drury Lane is home to the "Man in Grey."

The Spaniards Inn and the Savoy Hotel are two more locations that have fascinating histories and are said to be haunted by various spirits. The Old Bailey, London's famous courthouse, is also said to be haunted by the ghosts of those who were sentenced to death there.

Overall, London's haunted history is a rich tapestry of stories, legends, and eerie experiences. Whether you believe in ghosts or not, the tales of London's haunted past are sure to intrigue and entertain anyone who's interested in the paranormal. So, let's get ready to explore London's top ten haunted places and uncover the mysteries that lie within!

In this book, we're going to explore the top ten haunted places in London, and I'm excited to share with you why these locations are considered some of the most haunted places in the city.

First, let's talk about the criteria for selecting these top ten locations. We looked for places that had a rich history, a reputation for being haunted, and had numerous reports of ghostly sightings and paranormal activity. These are the places where people have reported feeling a chill in the air, seeing strange apparitions, or hearing unexplained noises.

GHOSTS OF LONDON: TEN HAUNTED PLACES IN THE CITY

Now, let's get to the good stuff! The Tower of London is at the top of our list because it has a history of torture, executions, and murder. It's said that the ghosts of the executed prisoners still haunt the tower, with the White Lady and the headless ghost being the most famous of the apparitions. Highgate Cemetery is another location that made the cut because it's said to be home to the "Highgate Vampire" and has been the site of numerous reports of ghostly sightings.

The London Dungeon, Viaduct Tavern, and Grenadier Pub are all known for their ghostly patrons. The Bank of England is said to be haunted by a ghostly figure known as the "Black Nun," while the Theatre Royal, Drury Lane is home to the "Man in Grey." The Spaniards Inn and the Savoy Hotel both have fascinating histories and are said to be haunted by various spirits, including former guests and even a highwayman.

Finally, the Old Bailey rounds out our list because of its legal significance and numerous reports of ghostly sightings over the years. It's said that the ghosts of those who were sentenced to death at the courthouse still linger in the building, and many people have reported feeling a chill in the air or seeing apparitions while inside.

So there you have it, I hope you're excited to explore each of these locations and learn more about the ghosts and spirits that are said to haunt them.

EDWARD TURNER

Chapter 1: The Tower of London

Historical background of the Tower of London

Ah, the fascinating history of the Tower of London! This iconic fortress has been a part of London's skyline for over 900 years and has played a pivotal role in the city's history.

The Tower of London was built in 1066 by William the Conqueror, shortly after his victory at the Battle of Hastings. Initially, it was a wooden structure built to keep control over the city of London and to protect the newly established Norman monarchy. Over time, the tower was rebuilt and expanded, with new additions being made throughout the centuries.

One of the most well-known uses of the Tower of London was as a prison. From the 12th century to the 20th century, the tower was used to house prisoners, including high-profile figures such as Anne Boleyn, Queen Elizabeth I, and Sir Walter Raleigh. Many prisoners were executed within the walls of the tower, and their ghosts are said to haunt the fortress to this day.

The Tower of London also served as a royal residence for many monarchs throughout history. It was during the Tudor period that the tower was expanded and transformed into a lavish palace. King Henry VIII even had a tennis court built within the walls of the tower, which is still in use today!

Another intriguing aspect of the Tower of London's history is its use as a treasury. The tower was home to the Crown Jewels of England, which were kept within its walls for safekeeping. The Crown Jewels include some of the most impressive and valuable pieces of jewellery in the world, including the Imperial State Crown, which is adorned with over 2,800 diamonds!

One of the most unique features of the Tower of London is its resident ravens. According to legend, if the ravens were to leave the tower, then the kingdom would fall. To prevent this from happening, the ravens are fed and cared for by the Yeoman Warders, who are also known as Beefeaters.

Today, the Tower of London is a popular tourist attraction, drawing millions of visitors each year. It's not hard to see why, as the tower is steeped in history and has a wealth of stories to tell. Visitors can explore the various towers and chambers, learn about the prisoners who were once held within its walls, and even see the Crown Jewels up close.

The Tower of London is a fascinating piece of English history that has played a significant role in the country's past. From its origins as a wooden fortress to its use as a royal residence and treasury, the tower has a rich and varied history that has been shaped by the people who have called it home. So why not pay a visit and discover the secrets of the Tower of London for yourself?

The most famous ghostly sightings

WHEN IT COMES TO HAUNTED places in London, the Tower of London is undoubtedly one of the most famous. Its long history, including its use as a royal palace, a prison, and a place of execution, has left behind a legacy of ghostly sightings and eerie stories.

One of the most famous ghostly sightings at the Tower of London is that of the White Lady. According to legend, the White Lady is the ghost of Queen Anne Boleyn, the second wife of King Henry VIII, who was executed at the Tower in 1536. Over the years, there have been countless reports of the White Lady appearing to visitors at the Tower, often near the site of her execution.

Many of those who claim to have seen the White Lady describe her as wearing a white gown and carrying her severed head in her hands. Some even say that she glows with an otherworldly light, adding to the eerie atmosphere of the Tower. While sceptics may dismiss these sightings as nothing more than stories or tricks of the mind, many visitors to the Tower remain convinced that the White Lady is real and continues to haunt the place where she met her tragic end.

Another famous ghostly sighting at the Tower of London is that of the headless ghost. This spectral figure is said to be the ghost of Sir Walter Raleigh, a famous explorer and poet who was imprisoned in the Tower for 13 years. According to legend, Sir Walter was beheaded in the Tower's courtyard in 1618, and his ghost has been seen wandering the Tower's grounds ever since.

Those who claim to have seen the headless ghost describe him as wearing old-fashioned clothing and carrying his severed head under his arm. Some say that he appears at night, while others claim to have seen him during the day. While the veracity of these sightings is up for debate, the legend of the headless ghost remains one of the Tower's most enduring ghost stories.

Of course, these are just two examples of the many ghostly sightings that have been reported at the Tower of London over the years. From the ghost of King Henry VI to the apparition of a bear that once lived in the Tower's menagerie, there is no shortage of eerie tales to be found at this historic site.

Whether you believe in ghosts or not, there is no denying the power of these stories to capture the imagination and send shivers down the spine. If you're brave enough to visit the Tower of London yourself, be sure to keep your eyes open for any spectral visitors who may be lurking in the shadows. Who knows – you may just have your own ghostly sighting to add to the Tower's long list of eerie tales.

Theories about the ghosts' origins and motivations

THE EXISTENCE OF GHOSTS and the paranormal has been a subject of fascination for centuries, and the Tower of London is no exception. Theories abound as to the origins and motivations of the ghosts that are said to haunt this famous site. Let's take a closer look at some of the most common theories.

One theory is that the ghosts are the spirits of people who suffered violent or traumatic deaths at the Tower. This theory certainly has some merit, given the Tower's long and often bloody history. From the execution of Anne Boleyn to the torture and murder of prisoners during the reign of Queen Elizabeth I, the Tower has seen more than its fair share of death and violence. According to this theory, the spirits of those who died in such a gruesome manner are unable to find peace and are doomed to roam the halls of the Tower for eternity.

Another theory is that the ghosts are simply residual energy left behind by past events. This theory suggests that the traumatic events that took place at the Tower have left an imprint on the environment, which can be picked up by sensitive individuals. In other words, the ghosts aren't really spirits at all, but rather the lingering energy of past events that have been imprinted on the environment.

Some people believe that the ghosts at the Tower are simply a figment of people's imagination, a product of suggestion and the power of the mind. According to this theory, people hear stories about the Tower's ghosts and become so convinced that they are real that they start to see and hear things that aren't really there. This theory is often used to explain away paranormal activity in general, but it's worth noting that many of the reports of ghostly sightings at the Tower come from credible witnesses who had no prior knowledge of the Tower's haunted history.

Finally, there are those who believe that the ghosts at the Tower are malevolent spirits, intent on causing harm to the living. This theory suggests that the ghosts are not simply trapped souls, but rather entities with their own motivations and desires. Some people believe that these malevolent spirits are the result of dark magic or other supernatural forces, while others believe that they are simply the product of the negative energy that has built up at the Tower over the centuries.

Of course, there are countless other theories about the ghosts at the Tower, ranging from the plausible to the downright outlandish. Ultimately, the truth is likely a combination of all of these theories and more. The human mind is a complex thing, and the world of the paranormal is even more so. While we may never know the full truth about the ghosts at the Tower, we can continue to be fascinated by their stories and the mysteries that surround them. Whether you believe in ghosts or not, there's no denying that the Tower of London is a place with a rich and fascinating history, and one that continues to capture the imaginations of people around the world.

Personal accounts of ghostly experiences

THE PERSONAL ACCOUNTS of ghostly experiences at the Tower of London are both intriguing and eerie. Many visitors to the Tower have reported encountering ghostly apparitions, hearing unexplained noises, and feeling a sense of unease in certain areas of the castle. Let's take a closer look at some of these accounts.

One of the most famous ghostly sightings at the Tower is that of the White Lady. The White Lady is believed to be the ghost of Arbella Stuart, a cousin of King James I who was imprisoned in the Tower in 1611. According to legend, Arbella was imprisoned in a room near the chapel and was eventually left to die of starvation. Visitors to the Tower have reported seeing a ghostly woman dressed in white roaming the corridors of the Tower, particularly in the area near the chapel. Some have even reported feeling a cold breath on the back of their necks, as if someone was standing right behind them.

Another famous ghostly sighting at the Tower is that of the headless ghost. The headless ghost is believed to be that of Anne Boleyn, the second wife of King Henry VIII, who was executed at the Tower in 1536. According to legend, Anne's ghost appears on the anniversary of her execution, dressed in a white gown and carrying her severed head. Visitors to the Tower have reported seeing a ghostly figure dressed in Tudor-era clothing, with no head on their shoulders, wandering the grounds of the Tower.

One particularly eerie personal account comes from a former guard at the Tower, who reported seeing a ghostly apparition in the chapel. According to the guard, he was standing in the chapel late one night when he heard the sound of footsteps coming towards him. When he turned around, he saw a figure dressed in 16th-century clothing walking towards him. The guard described the figure as having a "ghostly, translucent quality," and reported feeling a sense of fear and unease. The figure disappeared as suddenly as it had appeared, leaving the guard shaken and unnerved.

Another personal account comes from a group of tourists who visited the Tower late at night. The group reported hearing strange noises coming from one of the towers, including the sound of heavy breathing and footsteps. They also reported feeling a sense of unease and fear, as if they were being watched by someone or something. When they investigated the tower, they found no one inside, but reported feeling a sudden drop in temperature as they entered the room.

These personal accounts, along with countless others, demonstrate the widespread belief in the ghostly presence at the Tower of London. While some may dismiss these experiences as mere legends and stories, others argue that they provide compelling evidence of the existence of the paranormal. Whether you believe in ghosts or not, there is no denying the fascination and intrigue that surrounds the Tower of London and its haunted history.

GHOSTS OF LONDON: TEN HAUNTED PLACES IN THE CITY

Chapter 2: Highgate Cemetery

History of Highgate Cemetery

Highgate Cemetery is a historic cemetery located in North London. It was opened in 1839 and quickly became one of the most prestigious cemeteries in the city. Today, it is a popular tourist destination and a notable site for paranormal activity. The cemetery is divided into two parts: the East Cemetery, which is open to the public, and the West Cemetery, which can only be accessed by guided tour.

The cemetery is famous for its Gothic architecture and impressive monuments, including the Circle of Lebanon, a towering cedar tree that has become a symbol of the cemetery. But Highgate Cemetery is also famous for its notable inhabitants. Many famous individuals have been buried there, including authors, scientists, and even Karl Marx.

One of the most famous graves in Highgate Cemetery is that of Douglas Adams, author of "The Hitchhiker's Guide to the Galaxy." His grave is adorned with a metal plaque in the shape of a towel, a nod to his famous book. Another famous grave is that of George Eliot, author of "Middlemarch." Her grave is marked with a simple headstone that reads "Mary Ann Cross" instead of her pen name.

Highgate Cemetery is also known for its association with the Highgate Vampire. In the 1970s, there were reports of a vampire-like figure lurking in the cemetery. The legend gained widespread attention and led to numerous vampire hunters descending on the cemetery in search of the creature. While there is no evidence that the Highgate Vampire ever existed, the legend lives on and continues to attract visitors to the cemetery.

One of the most interesting aspects of Highgate Cemetery is its history. When it was opened in 1839, it was intended to be a burial place for the elite of Victorian society. The cemetery was designed to be a peaceful and beautiful final resting place, with carefully landscaped gardens and ornate memorials. But as the cemetery became more popular, it began to attract a wider range of people.

Over time, the cemetery fell into disrepair and became overgrown. Many of the graves were damaged or vandalised, and the cemetery became a haven for drug users and other unsavoury characters. In the 1970s, a group of concerned locals formed the Friends of Highgate Cemetery to help restore the cemetery and prevent further damage.

Today, Highgate Cemetery is a protected site and a popular tourist destination. The cemetery is a unique window into the past, with graves and monuments that tell the stories of some of the most fascinating individuals in history. Whether you're a history buff, a literature lover, or simply looking for a spooky adventure, Highgate Cemetery is a must-visit destination in London.

The infamous "Highgate Vampire" legend

HIGHGATE CEMETERY IN North London is a site steeped in history, with many tales of tragedy and mystery. One of the most enduring legends associated with this cemetery is that of the "Highgate Vampire," which has fascinated and frightened people for decades.

The story of the Highgate Vampire began in the late 1960s and early 1970s, a time when many people in England were fascinated by the supernatural. It was during this time that a number of people began to report seeing a tall, dark figure with glowing eyes lurking around the cemetery.

Rumours quickly spread that the figure was a vampire, and many people in the area became frightened. Some even claimed to have seen the creature attack people or animals, leaving them drained of blood.

As the legend grew, a number of groups began to form in an effort to track down and destroy the vampire. Some of these groups were made up of self-proclaimed vampire hunters, who claimed to have knowledge of ancient rituals and weapons that could be used to defeat the creature.

The hysteria surrounding the Highgate Vampire reached its peak in March 1970, when a group of people entered the cemetery armed with stakes, crosses, and other weapons. They claimed to have seen the vampire and were intent on destroying it.

The situation quickly spiralled out of control, with the group vandalising graves and causing damage to the cemetery. The police were eventually called in to restore order, and a number of people were arrested.

Despite the hysteria and damage caused by the vampire hunters, there is little evidence to suggest that there was ever a real vampire in Highgate Cemetery. Many experts believe that the sightings and reports of attacks were simply the result of overactive imaginations and a desire to believe in something supernatural.

However, the Highgate Vampire legend lives on to this day, with many people still fascinated by the idea of a bloodthirsty creature lurking in the shadows of the cemetery.

In addition to the vampire legend, Highgate Cemetery is also known for its many notable inhabitants. The cemetery was opened in 1839, and quickly became a popular burial site for London's wealthy and influential residents.

Some of the cemetery's most famous residents include Karl Marx, the famous philosopher and political theorist, and Douglas Adams, the author of "The Hitchhiker's Guide to the Galaxy." Other notable residents include George Eliot, author of "Middlemarch," and Alexander Litvinenko, a former Russian spy who was poisoned in London in 2006.

Today, Highgate Cemetery is a popular tourist attraction and a site of historical interest. Visitors can explore the cemetery's beautiful Gothic architecture, as well as the graves of its many famous residents. The cemetery also offers guided tours, which provide a fascinating glimpse into the cemetery's rich history and the stories of the people buried there.

Whether you believe in the legend of the Highgate Vampire or not, there is no denying that Highgate Cemetery is a site of great historical and cultural significance. Its stunning architecture and fascinating stories continue to attract visitors from all over the world, and its legacy as a final resting place for some of London's most influential figures is a testament to its enduring importance.

Personal accounts of ghostly experiences

HIGHGATE CEMETERY IS known to be one of the most haunted places in London. Its eerie atmosphere and gothic architecture make it the perfect location for ghostly sightings and strange occurrences. Over the years, there have been many personal accounts of ghostly experiences at Highgate Cemetery, adding to the legend and mystery of this iconic London landmark.

One of the most commonly reported ghostly sightings at Highgate Cemetery is the figure of a woman in white. She is often seen wandering through the cemetery, wearing a long white dress and a veil. Many visitors to the cemetery have reported seeing her, and she is believed to be the ghost of a woman who was buried at the cemetery in the early 1900s. Her identity is unknown, but her ghostly presence is still felt today.

Another famous ghostly experience at Highgate Cemetery is the strange phenomenon known as the "Vanishing Circle." This mysterious occurrence involves a circle of trees in the cemetery that is said to disappear and reappear at random intervals. Visitors have reported walking past the circle and then turning back to find that it has disappeared. Others have reported seeing the circle one minute and then turning back to find it gone the next. This strange phenomenon has never been fully explained and remains a mystery to this day.

In addition to these sightings, there have been numerous reports of strange noises and unexplained movements in the cemetery. Some visitors have reported hearing footsteps or whispers, while others have seen objects move on their own. There have also been reports of strange smells and temperature changes, as well as the feeling of being watched by an unseen presence.

One particularly chilling account comes from a group of paranormal investigators who visited the cemetery in 2013. While conducting an investigation, they captured what they believe to be the voice of a ghostly child on their audio recorder. The voice is faint, but can be heard saying "Hello." The investigators were unable to explain the source of the voice and believe it to be evidence of a ghostly presence in the cemetery.

Another group of visitors reported seeing a ghostly figure of a man walking through the cemetery. They described him as wearing a long coat and a top hat, and he appeared to be walking with purpose towards a specific grave. When they approached the grave, they found that it belonged to a man who had died in the early 1800s. The ghostly figure has never been identified, but his presence is still felt in the cemetery today.

Despite the many ghostly sightings and experiences reported at Highgate Cemetery, there are still sceptics who believe that these phenomena can be explained by natural occurrences or psychological factors. However, for those who have had personal experiences at the cemetery, there is no doubt that something otherworldly is at play.

Whether you believe in ghosts or not, there is no denying the eerie and haunting atmosphere of Highgate Cemetery. Its history and architecture make it a popular destination for tourists and ghost hunters alike, and the personal accounts of ghostly experiences only add to its mystique.

Modern-day sightings and investigations

HIGHGATE CEMETERY IS not only known for its historical significance and notable inhabitants, but it has also gained a reputation for being one of the most haunted places in London. Over the years, many people have reported experiencing strange and unexplained phenomena while visiting the cemetery.

One of the most common reported sightings in the cemetery is that of a tall figure, dressed in a long coat, top hat, and with piercing eyes. This figure is said to move silently and quickly through the cemetery, often disappearing without a trace. Some people have reported feeling an intense feeling of unease or even terror when encountering this figure, leading many to speculate that it could be the ghost of one of the cemetery's famous residents.

One of the most well-known sightings at Highgate Cemetery occurred in the late 1960s and early 1970s. During this time, several people reported seeing a tall, dark figure with glowing red eyes in the cemetery. This figure was often described as being around seven feet tall and was said to move incredibly quickly, disappearing into the shadows before anyone could get a good look at it.

These sightings led to a surge of interest in the cemetery and the development of the "Highgate Vampire" legend. Some people speculated that the figure was a vampire, rising from the dead to terrorise the living. Others believed it to be a demonic entity or even a ghost.

The legend of the Highgate Vampire led to many people visiting the cemetery in hopes of encountering the creature. Some even claimed to have found evidence of its existence, such as animal carcasses drained of blood or strange markings on gravestones. However, there is no concrete evidence to support the existence of a vampire or any other supernatural entity in the cemetery.

Despite this, paranormal investigators have continued to visit the cemetery in hopes of uncovering evidence of ghostly activity. Some have used equipment such as EMF metres, thermal cameras, and audio recording devices to try and capture evidence of paranormal activity. Others have used more traditional methods, such as séances or attempting to communicate with spirits through Ouija boards.

In recent years, there have been several reported sightings and experiences at the cemetery. In 2009, a group of tourists reported seeing a figure in Victorian clothing walking through the cemetery. They claimed that the figure disappeared into thin air before their eyes.

In 2015, a paranormal investigator reported feeling a strange presence in the cemetery and captured a photograph that appears to show a ghostly figure standing in the background. While some have dismissed this as a trick of the light, others believe that it could be evidence of the cemetery's ghostly inhabitants.

There have also been reports of strange sounds and disembodied voices in the cemetery, as well as the feeling of being watched or followed. Some visitors have reported feeling a sudden drop in temperature or a strange sensation of pressure on their bodies, which they believe to be the presence of a ghostly entity.

Despite the many reported sightings and experiences at Highgate Cemetery, there is still no conclusive evidence to prove the existence of ghosts or other supernatural entities. However, the cemetery remains a popular destination for paranormal enthusiasts and curious visitors alike, and the stories and legends surrounding it continue to capture the imaginations of people around the world.

EDWARD TURNER

Chapter 3: The London Dungeon

The history of the London Dungeon

Welcome to the dark and eerie world of the London Dungeon, where history meets horror.

The London Dungeon is a popular tourist attraction located in the heart of London, near the London Eye and the River Thames. It was opened in 1974 and was originally designed to educate visitors about the gruesome history of London in a unique and interactive way.

The idea behind the London Dungeon was to bring history to life through live performances and special effects. The attraction takes visitors on a journey through time, from the Roman invasion of Britain to the Jack the Ripper murders and beyond. It aims to show visitors what life was like in the past, including the dark and horrifying aspects that are often overlooked in traditional history books.

The London Dungeon is housed in the historic County Hall building, which was built in 1922 and was the seat of the London County Council until 1986. The building is a Grade II listed building and has been beautifully restored to preserve its original features.

The original London Dungeon was much smaller than the current attraction and only covered a few rooms in the basement of the County Hall building. However, over the years, the attraction has expanded to cover a larger area, and new exhibits and shows have been added to keep visitors coming back for more.

Today, the London Dungeon covers an area of over 20,000 square feet and includes over 40 different shows and exhibits. Some of the most popular exhibits include the Traitor's Gate, the Torture Chamber, and the Great Fire of London. Visitors can also experience live shows featuring some of the most notorious characters from London's history, such as Sweeney Todd, the barber who murdered his clients and turned them into meat pies.

One of the unique features of the London Dungeon is its use of special effects and technology to enhance the visitor experience. The attraction uses state-of-the-art sound and lighting systems, as well as animatronics and 360-degree sets, to create an immersive and realistic environment.

In addition to its educational and entertainment purposes, the London Dungeon has also been used as a filming location for movies and TV shows. Some of the most notable productions that have used the London Dungeon as a location include the movie "From Hell," which is based on the Jack the Ripper murders, and the TV series "Doctor Who."

The London Dungeon has become a must-see attraction for visitors to London who are looking for a unique and thrilling experience. It has won numerous awards and accolades over the years, including the Best UK Attraction award at the British Travel Awards in 2019.

The London Dungeon is a fascinating and unique attraction that offers visitors a glimpse into the darker side of London's history. It has grown from a small basement exhibit to a massive and immersive experience that combines history, entertainment, and horror. Whether you are a history buff or just looking for a thrilling adventure, the London Dungeon is a must-see attraction that is sure to leave a lasting impression.

The most famous ghostly sightings

THE LONDON DUNGEON is a popular tourist attraction that recreates the city's dark and sinister past through interactive exhibits and live performances. Visitors can expect to be taken on a journey through various eras of London's history, from the Roman invasion to the Great Fire of 1666, and learn about some of the city's most infamous characters, such as Jack the Ripper and Sweeney Todd. With such a macabre focus, it's no surprise that the London Dungeon is also rumoured to be one of the most haunted locations in the city, with numerous reported sightings of ghosts and other paranormal activity.

One of the most famous ghostly sightings at the London Dungeon is that of Anne Boleyn, the second wife of King Henry VIII. Anne was famously beheaded at the Tower of London in 1536, and her ghost is said to have been seen wandering the grounds of the London Dungeon. Visitors have reported seeing a woman in Tudor-era clothing with long dark hair, believed to be Anne, walking through the exhibits or standing in corners, watching them. Some visitors have even claimed to have felt a cold breeze or a sense of unease when in her presence.

Another popular ghostly sighting at the London Dungeon is that of Jack the Ripper. The notorious serial killer who terrorised London in the late 1800s is said to haunt the exhibit that focuses on his crimes. Visitors have reported feeling a chill in the air or catching a glimpse of a shadowy figure in the corner of their eye while touring the exhibit. Some have even claimed to have heard whispering or footsteps that seem to follow them.

The London Dungeon also has an exhibit dedicated to the infamous "Black Plague" that devastated London in the 14th century. Visitors are transported to a recreated version of the city during the time of the outbreak, complete with dim lighting and creepy sound effects. It's no surprise that this exhibit has also been the site of numerous reported ghostly sightings. Visitors have reported feeling a cold breath on their necks or hearing coughing and wheezing sounds, as if someone is sick and struggling to breathe. Some have even claimed to have seen ghostly apparitions of plague victims wandering through the exhibit.

In addition to these specific sightings, visitors to the London Dungeon have reported a general sense of unease and feeling as though they are being watched throughout their visit. Some have claimed to feel a cold breeze or a sudden drop in temperature, even on warm days. Others have reported seeing unexplainable shadows or hearing strange noises, such as footsteps or whispering, that seem to come from nowhere.

The London Dungeon has been the site of numerous paranormal investigations over the years, with many investigators attempting to capture evidence of the reported hauntings. Some have used electromagnetic field (EMF) metres to detect fluctuations in the electromagnetic field, which is believed to be a sign of paranormal activity. Others have used audio recorders to capture electronic voice phenomena (EVPs), which are unexplained voices or sounds that are believed to be the result of paranormal activity. While there has been some evidence captured, the hauntings at the London Dungeon remain largely unexplained.

Overall, the London Dungeon is a fascinating attraction that offers visitors a glimpse into London's dark and gruesome past. However, those with a fear of the paranormal may want to think twice before visiting, as the reported ghostly sightings and other paranormal activity may give them more than they bargained for.

Theories about the nature of the hauntings

THE LONDON DUNGEON is known for its chilling recreations of some of the city's most gruesome historical events, including the Great Fire of London, Jack the Ripper's murders, and the Plague. But in addition to the live actors and special effects, visitors have reported a number of unexplained experiences, leading many to believe that the Dungeon is truly haunted.

So what could be causing these ghostly sightings and paranormal experiences? There are several theories about the nature of the hauntings at the London Dungeon.

One possibility is that the spirits of those who suffered and died during the events being portrayed in the attraction remain trapped there, unable to move on. For example, in the Jack the Ripper exhibit, visitors have reported feeling a sense of unease and even feeling as though they were being watched. Some believe this could be the spirit of one of Jack the Ripper's victims, still haunting the area where she was killed.

Another theory is that the intense emotions and energy created by the performances and special effects at the London Dungeon could be attracting and/or creating paranormal activity. This is sometimes referred to as the "stone tape theory," which suggests that buildings and other physical objects can absorb and hold onto the energy of past events and emotions. In the case of the London Dungeon, the high level of fear, anxiety, and other intense emotions created by the attraction's experiences may be leaving a lasting impression on the environment, creating a kind of "residual haunting" that visitors can sense.

There are also those who believe that the London Dungeon is simply built on top of an area that has a high level of paranormal activity. This could be due to ley lines, which are said to be lines of energy that run through the earth and can have an impact on the environment and those who inhabit it. It's possible that the London Dungeon was constructed over one of these ley lines, leading to an increase in paranormal activity.

Despite the various theories, the exact nature of the hauntings at the London Dungeon remains a mystery. What is clear, however, is that many visitors have reported unexplained experiences while at the attraction. Whether it's feeling a cold spot or seeing a figure in the shadows, these experiences continue to fascinate and terrify those who visit the London Dungeon.

Personal accounts of ghostly experiences

THE LONDON DUNGEON is one of the most popular tourist attractions in the city, offering visitors a chance to experience some of the darker moments in London's history. However, it is not just the exhibits that attract people to the Dungeon - many visitors report eerie and unsettling experiences, indicating that the place may be haunted.

There are numerous personal accounts of ghostly experiences at the London Dungeon, including sightings of apparitions, strange noises, and unexplained smells. One of the most commonly reported sightings is that of a ghostly figure known as the "Grey Lady." She is said to appear in the corridors of the Dungeon, wearing a long, grey dress and a white bonnet. Witnesses describe feeling an overwhelming sense of sadness and despair when they see her, leading some to believe that she may have been a prisoner or victim of torture in the past.

Another reported ghostly sighting is that of a spectral figure known as "Jack the Ripper." This notorious serial killer terrorised London in the late 19th century and is said to haunt the London Dungeon to this day. Visitors have reported seeing his ghostly figure lurking in the shadows, or even feeling his cold breath on their necks. Some speculate that he is drawn to the Dungeon due to its exhibits about his gruesome crimes.

Visitors to the London Dungeon have also reported experiencing unexplained phenomena such as sudden temperature drops, footsteps and whispers when no one else is around, and objects moving on their own. Many of these experiences occur in the exhibits themselves, adding an extra layer of terror to the already spine-chilling displays.

So, what could be the explanation for these ghostly experiences at the London Dungeon? Some believe that the building itself may be haunted, as it was built on the site of an ancient plague pit. Others suggest that the intense emotions and fear experienced by visitors in the exhibits may somehow create a paranormal energy that attracts spirits.

Another theory is that the spirits of those who suffered and died in the gruesome events depicted in the exhibits may still be present and haunting the Dungeon. Given the Dungeon's focus on torture, executions, and other gruesome events, it is not hard to imagine that the site could be a magnet for negative energy.

Despite the numerous reported sightings and experiences, the management of the London Dungeon has remained sceptical of the paranormal. They maintain that the experiences are simply part of the attraction's immersive experience, designed to scare visitors and create an atmosphere of terror.

However, for those who have had personal encounters with the supernatural at the London Dungeon, the experiences are very real and unforgettable. Whether the haunting is a product of the building's history or simply the power of suggestion, it is clear that the London Dungeon is a place that can chill visitors to the bone - even without any actual ghosts.

Chapter 4: The Viaduct Tavern

The history of the Viaduct Tavern

The Viaduct Tavern is a historic pub located in the heart of London. It is situated in a stunning Victorian building that was constructed in the late 19th century. The pub has a rich and fascinating history, with many notable patrons over the years.

The building that houses the Viaduct Tavern was originally constructed in 1875 as a gin palace, which was a type of public house that specialises in serving gin. In the early 20th century, the pub became a popular haunt for London's legal professionals, who worked in the nearby courts and offices. In fact, the pub is located just a few steps away from the Old Bailey, which is the most famous criminal court in the country.

Over the years, the Viaduct Tavern has attracted a number of notable patrons. One of the most famous was the novelist Charles Dickens, who is said to have been a regular visitor to the pub. Dickens was known to be a fan of gin, and he may have enjoyed a tipple or two at the Viaduct Tavern during his visits to the area.

Another notable patron of the pub was the infamous gangster Reggie Kray. Kray was a notorious figure in the London criminal underworld during the 1960s, and he was known to frequent the Viaduct Tavern on a regular basis. In fact, it is said that Kray used to use the pub as a meeting place for his criminal associates.

Despite its rich history and fascinating patrons, the Viaduct Tavern has not always been a popular destination for visitors. In the 20th century, the pub fell into disrepair and became known for its rowdy and often violent clientele. However, in recent years, the pub has been lovingly restored and is once again a popular destination for locals and tourists alike.

One of the most striking features of the Viaduct Tavern is its stunning Victorian interior. The pub is decorated in the style of a traditional Victorian gin palace, with high ceilings, ornate plasterwork, and stained glass windows. The bar itself is made of polished mahogany, and there are several cosy booths and private rooms where patrons can enjoy a quiet drink.

Another notable feature of the pub is its underground cellar, which is said to be haunted. According to legend, the cellar was once used as a holding cell for prisoners who were awaiting trial at the nearby Old Bailey. It is said that the ghosts of these prisoners still haunt the cellar to this day, and that visitors to the pub have reported feeling a cold presence or hearing strange noises while they are down there.

Overall, the Viaduct Tavern is a fascinating and historic pub that is well worth a visit. Whether you're a fan of Victorian architecture, London's legal history, or just a good pint of beer, there is something for everyone at this iconic London pub.

The most famous ghostly sightings

THE VIADUCT TAVERN, located in the City of London, is a historic pub that dates back to the 19th century. It is widely known for its connection to the ghostly sightings and paranormal experiences that have been reported by both staff and patrons over the years.

One of the most famous ghostly sightings at the Viaduct Tavern is that of a young girl who has been seen in the cellar. She is believed to be the ghost of a former resident who tragically died in a fire that occurred in the building next door. Some people have reported feeling her presence even when they cannot see her.

Another ghostly figure that is often spotted in the pub is a man in Victorian clothing. He is usually seen standing at the bar or sitting at a table by himself. Some people believe that he may have been a regular patron in the past.

Other paranormal experiences reported at the Viaduct Tavern include strange noises, such as footsteps and banging, that cannot be explained by natural causes. Some have also reported feeling sudden drops in temperature, even in areas where there are no windows or doors.

One particularly eerie experience occurred when a group of builders were renovating the pub. They had been working in the cellar when they heard a woman's voice calling out for help. They searched the area but found no one there. Later, they discovered that there had been a well in that area many years ago, and it is believed that the voice they heard may have belonged to someone who had fallen down the well and died.

The ghostly activity at the Viaduct Tavern has been reported for many years, with some patrons even claiming to have seen apparitions that vanish before their eyes. The paranormal occurrences at the pub have made it a popular destination for ghost hunters and paranormal enthusiasts.

So, why does the ghostly activity persist at the Viaduct Tavern? There are many theories, with some believing that the spirits are attached to the building itself or to the surrounding area. Others believe that the spirits may be connected to the pub's long history, which includes serving as a debtor's prison and being located near the site of a former gallows.

Whatever the reason, the ghostly sightings and paranormal experiences at the Viaduct Tavern continue to intrigue and captivate those who visit the pub. Whether you're a sceptic or a believer in the supernatural, there is no denying the unique and eerie atmosphere that surrounds this historic London landmark.

Theories about the nature of the hauntings

THE VIADUCT TAVERN, located in London's financial district, is known not only for its historic charm and delicious food but also for its paranormal activity. Visitors to the tavern have reported several ghostly sightings and unexplained occurrences, leading to various theories about the nature of the hauntings.

One theory is that the Viaduct Tavern is haunted by the ghosts of former patrons who died tragically or violently. The tavern is over 150 years old and has seen its fair share of violence over the years. It was built on the site of a former prison, which was known for its inhumane conditions and executions. Additionally, the area was a popular spot for public hangings in the past. Some believe that the spirits of those who died in these gruesome ways have lingered on, unable to rest peacefully.

Another theory is that the hauntings are related to the tavern's location near the old Fleet River. The river was once a source of water for the city, but it also served as a dumping ground for waste and dead bodies. The river was eventually covered and turned into a sewer system, but some believe that the negative energy and history of the river continue to affect the area. The Viaduct Tavern is located near one of the old entrances to the Fleet sewer, which could explain the paranormal activity in the area.

Others believe that the hauntings are related to the history of the building itself. The Viaduct Tavern was built in 1875 and was originally a gin palace. It is known for its ornate Victorian decor and unique features, such as the separate entrances for men and women. Some speculate that the spirits of former patrons who enjoyed the gin palace and its lively atmosphere have chosen to linger on in the afterlife.

Finally, some believe that the hauntings are simply a result of the energy created by the building's long and eventful history. The Viaduct Tavern has seen many changes over the years, from its early days as a gin palace to its current role as a popular pub and restaurant. It has survived two World Wars and many other historic events. All of these experiences could have created a residual energy that continues to affect the building and its visitors.

Regardless of the theories, one thing is certain: the Viaduct Tavern is a hotspot for paranormal activity. Visitors have reported seeing ghostly apparitions, hearing unexplained footsteps and voices, and feeling sudden temperature changes. Some have even reported being touched or pushed by an unseen force.

These experiences are not limited to patrons and visitors, either. The staff at the Viaduct Tavern have also reported strange occurrences over the years. They have heard phantom footsteps and voices, seen objects move on their own, and felt sudden temperature drops in certain areas of the building.

Despite the spooky occurrences, the Viaduct Tavern remains a popular destination for locals and tourists alike. Whether you're interested in paranormal activity or just looking for a delicious meal and a pint of beer, the Viaduct Tavern has something for everyone. Who knows, you might even have your own ghostly encounter while you're there!

Personal accounts of ghostly experiences

THE VIADUCT TAVERN in London is a historic pub that has been in operation since 1869. As with many old buildings, the pub has a reputation for being haunted by several ghosts. Over the years, many people have reported strange experiences and sightings, making the pub a popular destination for ghost hunters and paranormal enthusiasts.

Personal accounts of ghostly experiences at the Viaduct Tavern are numerous and varied. Some people have reported seeing the apparition of a woman dressed in Victorian clothing standing in the corner of the pub's bar. Others have reported feeling a cold presence or hearing strange noises that they cannot explain.

One of the most common reports is the feeling of being touched or brushed past by an unseen presence. Many patrons have reported feeling a cold breeze or the sensation of someone running their fingers through their hair. Some people have even reported being pushed or shoved by an invisible force.

Several people have reported seeing the ghost of a man sitting in one of the pub's upstairs rooms. The man is said to be wearing old-fashioned clothing and is often seen smoking a pipe. He is sometimes seen staring out the window or walking around the room before disappearing.

Another ghostly presence reported at the Viaduct Tavern is that of a little girl. The girl is said to be around eight or nine years old and is often seen standing near the fireplace in the pub's back room. She is said to be wearing old-fashioned clothing and has long, curly hair. Some people have reported seeing her playing with a toy or giggling before disappearing.

In addition to these more prominent ghosts, there have been reports of other paranormal activity at the Viaduct Tavern. Some people have reported hearing strange noises or voices coming from the walls or ceiling. Others have reported feeling a sense of unease or a feeling of being watched.

Many theories have been put forward to explain the nature of these hauntings and why they persist. Some people believe that the ghosts are the spirits of former patrons or employees of the pub who have passed away. Others believe that the hauntings are the result of residual energy left behind by people who once lived or worked in the building.

Some people believe that the Viaduct Tavern's location near the site of an old Newgate prison may be a factor in the hauntings. It is thought that the building may be built on top of a former gallows or burial ground, which could explain the presence of so many ghosts.

Despite the many ghostly sightings and reports of paranormal activity at the Viaduct Tavern, the pub remains a popular destination for locals and visitors alike. Whether you believe in ghosts or not, there is no denying the pub's unique atmosphere and rich history. Whether you are looking for a pint of ale, a good meal, or a chance to experience the supernatural, the Viaduct Tavern is a must-visit destination for anyone interested in London's haunted history.

GHOSTS OF LONDON: TEN HAUNTED PLACES IN THE CITY

49

Chapter 5: The Grenadier Pub

History of the Grenadier Pub

The Grenadier Pub is a historic drinking establishment located in Belgravia, London. It was originally built in 1720 as the officer's mess for the First Regiment of Foot Guards and has since become a popular destination for both locals and tourists alike. The pub has a rich history and is closely tied to the military, with many of its decorations and artefacts dating back to its days as an officer's mess.

The building itself has a long and storied past. Originally, it was a coach house and stables, but was later converted into an officer's mess for the First Regiment of Foot Guards, which was stationed nearby at Wellington Barracks. During its time as an officer's mess, the Grenadier Pub was frequented by many notable figures, including members of the royal family and various military commanders.

One of the most famous stories associated with the Grenadier Pub involves a young soldier who was caught cheating at cards. As punishment, he was beaten to death by his fellow soldiers and his body was buried in the cellar of the pub. According to legend, his ghost still haunts the establishment, and visitors have reported seeing strange apparitions and feeling cold spots in the cellar.

Aside from its haunted history, the Grenadier Pub is also known for its military connections. The walls are adorned with various regimental crests and flags, and there are many historic artefacts on display, including a set of old military drums and a collection of muskets. The pub also hosts regular events for current and former members of the military, including reunion parties and commemorative ceremonies.

In addition to its military connections, the Grenadier Pub is also known for its excellent food and drink. The menu features classic British pub fare, including fish and chips, bangers and mash, and shepherd's pie, as well as a wide selection of beers and other libations. The pub's cosy interior and warm atmosphere make it a popular spot for both locals and tourists, and it has become something of an institution in the Belgravia area.

Overall, the Grenadier Pub is a unique and fascinating place with a long and storied history. Its military connections and haunted past make it an interesting destination for anyone interested in history or the paranormal, and its cosy atmosphere and excellent food and drink make it a popular spot for anyone looking to enjoy a night out in London. Whether you're a history buff, a ghost hunter, or just looking for a good meal and a pint, the Grenadier Pub is definitely worth a visit.

The most famous ghostly sightings

THE GRENADIER PUB IN London is not only known for its cosy atmosphere and excellent food and drink but also for its ghostly sightings and paranormal experiences. The pub is situated in the Belgravia district of London, and its history goes back over 200 years. The building was originally constructed in 1720 as the Duke of Wellington's officers' mess, and it is rumoured that the ghostly activity is related to its military past.

One of the most famous ghostly sightings at the Grenadier Pub is that of a young officer who is said to have been caught cheating at cards. According to legend, the officer was beaten to death by his fellow soldiers as punishment for his cheating. Many people have reported seeing the ghostly figure of the young officer dressed in his military uniform and walking around the pub.

Another ghostly presence that is often reported is that of a woman who is thought to have been a serving girl at the pub during the 19th century. According to legend, the serving girl was involved in an affair with a young officer who was stationed at the Grenadier Pub. When the officer was called away to war, the serving girl was left heartbroken and committed suicide by hanging herself in the pub's attic. Many visitors to the Grenadier Pub have reported hearing strange noises coming from the attic, and some have even claimed to have seen the ghostly figure of the serving girl.

In addition to the ghostly sightings, the Grenadier Pub is also known for its paranormal experiences. Many people have reported feeling an eerie presence throughout the building, and some have even claimed to have been touched by unseen hands. Strange sounds and voices have also been reported, particularly in the pub's cellar, which is said to have been used as a holding cell for prisoners during the 18th century.

Despite the numerous reports of ghostly sightings and paranormal experiences at the Grenadier Pub, there are many sceptics who believe that the stories are simply myths and legends. However, there are also many who swear by the authenticity of the ghostly sightings, and the pub's reputation as one of London's most haunted locations is firmly established.

So, what could be the reason behind the Grenadier Pub's ghostly sightings and paranormal experiences? One theory is that the pub's military past has left an imprint on the building, and the spirits of soldiers who died during their service are still present. It is also possible that the tragic stories of the young officer and serving girl have left a residual energy that continues to manifest itself as ghostly sightings.

Another theory is that the Grenadier Pub's location is significant. Belgravia is known for its history of duels, and it is possible that the spirits of those who died in these duels are still present in the area. Additionally, the Grenadier Pub is located near Hyde Park, which was once used as a site for public executions. It is possible that the spirits of those who were executed still linger in the area.

Regardless of the reason behind the ghostly sightings and paranormal experiences at the Grenadier Pub, they have certainly added to the pub's charm and allure. Whether you are a believer or a sceptic, a visit to the Grenadier Pub is sure to be a memorable experience. Who knows, you may even catch a glimpse of one of the pub's ghostly residents during your visit.

Theories about the nature of the hauntings

THE GRENADIER PUB IN London is known not only for its history and military connections but also for its ghostly sightings and paranormal experiences. Many theories have been put forth to explain the nature of the hauntings and why they persist to this day.

One theory is that the pub is haunted by the ghost of a young soldier who was flogged to death in the nearby courtyard. According to legend, the soldier was caught cheating at cards and was punished by his fellow soldiers. His ghost is said to haunt the upper floors of the pub, where he is often seen in full military uniform.

Another theory suggests that the pub is haunted by the ghost of a former landlord who was murdered in a brutal attack. The assailants were never caught, and the case remains unsolved to this day. Many patrons of the pub have reported seeing the ghost of the landlord, who is said to appear as a shadowy figure wearing a top hat and carrying a cane.

Some people believe that the hauntings are related to the pub's military connections. The Grenadier Pub was originally a officers' mess for the nearby barracks, and many soldiers frequented the pub during their time off. It is possible that the ghosts of former soldiers continue to haunt the pub, unable to leave their old haunt behind.

Others suggest that the Grenadier Pub is built on the site of an ancient burial ground, and that the hauntings are the result of disturbed spirits. The area was once a site of pagan worship, and it is possible that the pub is built on top of an ancient burial mound or sacred site. This theory is supported by the fact that many of the pub's ghostly sightings are of shadowy figures or orbs of light, which are often associated with spiritual activity.

Finally, some people believe that the Grenadier Pub is simply a place where the veil between the living and the dead is thin. They suggest that the pub's long history and the many lives that have passed through its doors have left a residual energy that is palpable to those who are sensitive to such things.

Regardless of the theories, one thing is certain: the Grenadier Pub is a place with a rich and fascinating history, and its ghostly sightings and paranormal experiences are part of what makes it such a unique and interesting destination for both locals and tourists alike. Whether you believe in ghosts or not, a visit to the Grenadier Pub is sure to be an unforgettable experience.

Personal accounts of ghostly experiences

THE GRENADIER PUB, located in the heart of London's Belgravia neighbourhood, has been a popular haunt for both locals and tourists for over two centuries. However, it is not just the delicious food and drinks that draw visitors to the

GHOSTS OF LONDON: TEN HAUNTED PLACES IN THE CITY

Grenadier. The pub is notorious for its supernatural activity, with many visitors reporting ghostly encounters during their visit.

Several personal accounts of ghostly experiences have been documented at the Grenadier over the years. One common experience reported by visitors is a sudden drop in temperature, accompanied by a feeling of unease. Many people have reported feeling an invisible presence or seeing objects move on their own. One of the most common sightings is of a young man who appears to be a soldier, dressed in a long coat and a tricorn hat. He is often seen standing by the fireplace or sitting at one of the tables, silently observing the patrons.

Another popular story associated with the Grenadier is the mysterious and inexplicable phenomena experienced by its employees. Many of the staff members have reported objects moving on their own, footsteps when no one is there, and even doors opening and closing by themselves. Several employees have also claimed to have seen the ghost of a woman dressed in Victorian-era clothing, who is believed to be the mistress of the Duke of Wellington.

One of the most intriguing stories associated with the Grenadier involves the mysterious curse placed on the pub. According to legend, the Grenadier was built on the site of a former military barracks where a young soldier was severely beaten to death after being caught cheating at cards. It is said that his ghost haunts the pub to this day, and visitors are warned not to mention his name, lest they incur his wrath.

Over the years, many theories have been put forward to explain the hauntings at the Grenadier. Some believe that the ghostly activity is a result of the pub's military connections, with the restless spirits of soldiers and officers who once frequented the establishment still lingering in the building. Others suggest that the pub's location on a ley line or other mystical energy field may be responsible for the unexplained phenomena.

Regardless of the explanation, the Grenadier remains a popular destination for those seeking a brush with the paranormal. The pub's unique atmosphere and rich history make it an intriguing place to visit, even for those who are not necessarily believers in the supernatural.

The Grenadier Pub is a fascinating location for anyone interested in the paranormal or the history of London. With its rich military history, mysterious curse, and numerous ghostly sightings, it is no wonder that this pub has become one of the most haunted locations in the city. Whether you are a sceptic or a believer, a visit to the Grenadier is sure to leave a lasting impression.

Chapter 6: The Bank of England

Historical background of the Bank of England

The Bank of England, also known as the "Old Lady of Threadneedle Street," is the central bank of the United Kingdom. Established in 1694, the Bank of England has a rich and fascinating history that spans centuries.

The Bank of England was founded in 1694 by a group of merchants who were concerned about the high cost of borrowing money from the government. The bank was established to provide the government with a stable source of funding, and to issue paper banknotes as a means of payment. At the time of its founding, the Bank of England was the only private bank in the country that was allowed to issue paper money.

The Bank of England played an important role in the development of the British economy in the 18th and 19th centuries. It helped to finance the industrial revolution, and it was instrumental in establishing the gold standard, which served as the basis for international currency exchange for much of the 19th and early 20th centuries.

During the First World War, the Bank of England played a key role in financing the war effort. It raised funds through the sale of government bonds and war savings certificates, and it helped to manage the country's foreign exchange reserves.

In the aftermath of the Second World War, the Bank of England was nationalised, and it became a public institution. It was given a new mandate to regulate the banking system and to control inflation. The bank's monetary policy committee was established in 1997, and it is responsible for setting interest rates in the UK.

In recent years, the Bank of England has played a central role in managing the British economy through a series of financial crises. During the global financial crisis of 2008, the bank implemented a series of measures to stabilise the financial system, including a program of quantitative easing and the establishment of a special lending facility for banks.

Today, the Bank of England is one of the most important institutions in the UK, and it continues to play a key role in the country's economic and financial affairs. Its primary objectives are to maintain price stability and to promote the stability of the financial system. It does this through a range of activities, including setting interest rates, regulating the banking system, and issuing banknotes.

The Bank of England has a rich and varied history that spans centuries. It has played a key role in the development of the British economy, and it continues to be an important institution today. Its history is intertwined with that of the UK, and its legacy can be felt in the financial and economic systems of the country. As such, the Bank of England remains a fascinating and important institution to this day.

The most famous ghostly sightings

THE BANK OF ENGLAND, as the central bank of the United Kingdom, has a rich and storied history dating back to its founding in 1694. Throughout its history, the bank has been the site of numerous ghostly sightings and paranormal experiences, making it a popular destination for those interested in the supernatural.

One of the most famous ghostly sightings at the Bank of England is that of the Black Nun. The story goes that in the 19th century, a nun was said to have been bricked up alive within the walls of the bank as punishment for an illicit affair with a banker. Ever since, her ghost has been seen wandering the halls and staircases of the bank. Some have even reported feeling a cold breeze and hearing the sound of her footsteps, despite being alone.

Another well-known ghostly figure at the Bank of England is the Old Lady. She is said to be the ghost of Sarah Whitehead, the sister of a stockbroker who, in the 18th century, lost all her money in a market crash and subsequently died of a broken heart. Her ghost has been reported to appear near the bank's garden, holding a bag of coins and weeping.

There are also reports of a ghostly figure known as the Banker. He is said to be the spirit of a former employee who hanged himself in the bank's rotunda. His ghost is said to appear in the bank's basement, often accompanied by a sense of unease and foreboding.

In addition to these well-known ghostly sightings, there have also been reports of ghostly apparitions, mysterious noises, and other paranormal activity at the Bank of England. Some have reported hearing the sound of ghostly laughter, while others have reported seeing the ghostly figure of a man in a top hat wandering the halls.

Despite the numerous reports of ghostly sightings and paranormal activity, the Bank of England has remained a functioning institution and is still in use today. However, many visitors to the bank report feeling an eerie sense of being watched, and some employees have even reported feeling a ghostly presence while working late at night.

The Bank of England has a long and fascinating history, and the numerous ghostly sightings and paranormal experiences associated with the institution only add to its mystique and allure. Whether you believe in ghosts or not, there is no denying the unique atmosphere of the bank and the sense of history and tradition that permeates its walls.

Theories about the ghosts' origins and motivations

THE BANK OF ENGLAND, with its long and storied history, is one of the most iconic buildings in London. As a result, it has been the subject of countless ghost stories and paranormal sightings over the years. There are several theories about the origins of these ghosts and why they persist within the walls of this historic institution.

One theory is that the ghosts are former employees of the bank who have returned to continue their work beyond the grave. According to this theory, these spirits are so devoted to their job and the institution they served that they cannot bear to leave it, even in death. Some believe that these ghosts may be former bank managers or other high-ranking officials who are still watching over the bank and ensuring that it continues to run smoothly.

Another theory is that the ghosts are the spirits of individuals who had dealings with the bank in life and have returned to seek revenge or justice. Some believe that these ghosts may be former customers or clients who were wronged by the bank in some way and are now seeking retribution for their mistreatment. Others believe that these spirits may be former employees who were mistreated or unfairly dismissed by the bank and are now seeking revenge on those who wronged them.

A third theory is that the ghosts are simply residual energy left over from the intense emotions and experiences that have taken place within the walls of the bank over the years. This theory suggests that the Bank of England has absorbed so much energy from the people and events that have taken place within it that it has become a kind of psychic sponge, soaking up and retaining the energy of the past. According to this theory, the ghosts that people see within the bank are simply the residual energy of past emotions and events that have become trapped within the building.

Regardless of the theory one subscribes to, there have been numerous reports of ghostly sightings and paranormal experiences within the Bank of England. For example, some people have reported seeing the ghost of a former bank manager wandering the halls of the bank, dressed in a Victorian-era suit and carrying a cane. Others have reported hearing strange noises, such as footsteps, voices, and even the sound of coins jingling.

One of the most famous ghostly sightings at the Bank of England is the ghost of Sarah Whitehead, who is said to haunt the bank's garden. Sarah Whitehead was the sister of a clerk at the bank who was executed for forgery in 1811. It is said that Sarah, grief-stricken over her brother's death, took her own life in the garden of the bank. Today, many people claim to have seen Sarah's ghost wandering through the garden, dressed in a white gown and weeping for her lost brother.

Another well-known ghostly sighting at the Bank of England is the ghost of a man known as "the black nun." According to legend, the black nun was a former employee of the bank who was caught stealing money and was subsequently sent to prison. After her release, she returned to the bank and killed herself by jumping from one of the upper floors. Today, people claim to see her ghost wandering through the halls of the bank, dressed in black and carrying a lantern.

Overall, the Bank of England has a long and fascinating history, with many stories and legends attached to it. While the origins of the bank's ghosts and paranormal experiences may never be fully understood, they continue to intrigue and captivate those who visit this iconic institution.

Personal accounts of ghostly experiences

THE BANK OF ENGLAND, with its long history and impressive architecture, is one of the most iconic landmarks in London. But beyond its financial significance, it is also known for being one of the most haunted buildings in the city. Over the years, there have been numerous reports of strange sightings and unexplained events that have occurred within its walls. Here are some personal accounts of ghostly experiences of the Bank of England.

One of the most well-known stories is that of the Bank's 'Black Nun.' According to legend, the nun was a former resident of a nearby convent who was in love with a banker who worked at the Bank of England. When her love was unrequited, the nun hanged herself from the rafters of the Bank's library. Since then, her ghost has been seen walking the halls, dressed in black with a white veil covering her face. There have also been reports of her voice being heard, and her cold presence felt in the room where she died.

Another famous story is that of the 'Banker's Ghost,' who is said to haunt the Bank's Garden Court. According to the tale, a banker who was conducting business in the Bank was assassinated, and his ghost has been seen ever since. The apparition is said to appear as a dark figure wearing a cloak and a wig, walking slowly along the halls before disappearing into thin air.

Several other ghosts have been reported at the Bank of England over the years. There have been sightings of a ghostly coach and horses, which are believed to have been involved in a fatal accident on the Bank's grounds. The apparition is said to appear suddenly, charging through the Bank's main gate before disappearing as quickly as it appeared.

Another spirit that is said to haunt the Bank is that of Sarah Whitehead, who was hanged for forgery in 1786. Her ghost is believed to roam the Bank's halls, muttering about her wrongful execution and seeking revenge against those who wronged her.

In addition to these stories, there have been reports of strange noises, doors slamming shut on their own, and other unexplained events. Some employees have reported feeling a sense of unease when working in certain areas of the Bank, particularly the old library and the underground vaults.

Despite the many reports of ghostly sightings and experiences at the Bank of England, there is no scientific evidence to support the existence of ghosts. However, believers in the paranormal continue to be drawn to the Bank, fascinated by the stories and the mysterious atmosphere that surrounds the building.

The Bank of England is not just a place of financial significance, but also a site of many ghostly experiences. The personal accounts of those who have worked or visited the Bank are testament to the enduring fascination with the supernatural and the enduring power of ghost stories. While sceptics may dismiss such accounts as mere legends or the result of an overactive imagination, there are those who swear by their veracity and continue to be captivated by the idea that the Bank of England is home to an array of restless spirits.

Chapter 7: The Theatre Royal, Drury Lane

The history of the Theatre Royal, Drury Lane

The Theatre Royal, Drury Lane is a historic theatre in London's West End. It has a rich and fascinating history, having hosted many famous productions and performers over the centuries. The theatre is known for its grandeur, beautiful architecture, and the many ghostly sightings that have been reported there over the years.

The original theatre on the site was built in 1663 by Thomas Killigrew, a playwright and theatre manager. It was called the Theatre Royal, Bridges Street, and was one of only two theatres in London at the time. The theatre was rebuilt in 1674 and again in 1775, when it was renamed the Theatre Royal, Drury Lane. The current building was constructed in 1812, after a fire destroyed the previous one.

Over the years, the Theatre Royal, Drury Lane has hosted many famous productions and performers. Some of the most well-known productions include the premieres of My Fair Lady, Oliver!, and Miss Saigon. Many famous actors have also performed at the theatre, including Laurence Olivier, Richard Burton, and Judi Dench.

The theatre's beautiful architecture is one of its main draws. The building is designed in the neoclassical style, with a grand facade and a beautiful interior. The auditorium is particularly impressive, with a large stage, ornate box seats, and a stunning chandelier. The theatre is also home to a number of beautiful murals, including a famous one by Thomas Gainsborough.

But perhaps the most famous aspect of the Theatre Royal, Drury Lane is its reputation for being haunted. There have been numerous ghostly sightings and paranormal experiences reported at the theatre over the years. Some of the most famous sightings include the ghost of Joseph Grimaldi, a famous clown who performed at the theatre in the 19th century. His ghost has been seen wandering the corridors, wearing his clown costume and makeup.

Another famous ghost is that of the Man in Grey, who is said to haunt the theatre's upper circle. The Man in Grey is believed to be the ghost of a man who was killed in a duel over a woman. He is often seen sitting in one of the theatre's seats, wearing a powdered wig and a grey suit.

There have also been reports of ghostly voices, strange smells, and unexplained cold spots throughout the theatre. Many people believe that the theatre is haunted by the ghosts of past performers and theatre-goers, who are still drawn to the building long after their deaths.

There are many theories about why the ghosts of the Theatre Royal, Drury Lane persist. Some people believe that they are attached to the building itself, and are unable to move on to the afterlife. Others believe that the ghosts are still drawn to the theatre because of the emotions and energy that are present during performances. Some people even believe that the theatre is built on a ley line, which is a powerful energy line that runs through the earth.

Whatever the reason for the haunting, there is no denying that the Theatre Royal, Drury Lane is a fascinating and spooky place. With its beautiful architecture and rich history, it is easy to see why so many people are drawn to the theatre – both in life and in death.

The most famous ghostly sightings

THE THEATRE ROYAL, Drury Lane, located in the heart of London's West End, is one of the oldest and most famous theatres in the world. With a history dating back over 350 years, it's no surprise that the theatre is also said to be haunted by a number of ghosts and spirits.

One of the most famous ghostly sightings at the Theatre Royal, Drury Lane, is the ghost of the "Man in Grey". According to legend, the Man in Grey was a young nobleman who was killed in a duel over a woman he loved. His ghost is said to haunt the theatre's upper circle, dressed in a grey cloak and a powdered wig. The Man in Grey has been seen by many people over the years, including actors, stagehands, and audience members.

Another famous ghostly sighting at the Theatre Royal, Drury Lane, is the ghost of the famous actor Charles Macklin. Macklin was known for his fiery temper, and he famously killed a fellow actor in a dispute over a wig. His ghost is said to haunt the theatre's green room, where he can be heard reciting lines from Shakespeare and other plays.

The theatre is also said to be haunted by the ghost of Joseph Grimaldi, a famous clown who was a regular performer at the theatre in the early 19th century. Grimaldi's ghost is said to appear in the dressing room that was once his, and he has been seen by many actors and stagehands over the years.

In addition to these famous ghostly sightings, the Theatre Royal, Drury Lane, is also said to be haunted by a number of other spirits. The ghost of a young girl has been seen in the theatre's upper circle, while the ghost of a stagehand who died during a performance in the 19th century is said to haunt the theatre's fly tower.

There have also been reports of strange noises, unexplained footsteps, and other ghostly occurrences throughout the theatre. Many people believe that the Theatre Royal, Drury Lane, is one of the most haunted buildings in London, and it has been the subject of numerous paranormal investigations over the years.

So why do these ghosts continue to haunt the Theatre Royal, Drury Lane? There are many theories, but most people believe that the theatre's long and colourful history is the main reason. With so many famous actors, playwrights, and other figures associated with the theatre over the years, it's no surprise that some of them may have left a spiritual imprint on the building.

Others believe that the Theatre Royal, Drury Lane, was built on a site that was already haunted, and that the spirits of previous occupants continue to linger there. Whatever the reason, there's no denying that the theatre is a place with a rich history and a vibrant, ghostly presence.

Despite the many ghostly sightings and paranormal experiences reported at the Theatre Royal, Drury Lane, the theatre remains a popular destination for theatregoers from around the world. Whether you believe in ghosts or not, there's no denying the theatre's unique and fascinating history, and its enduring place in the world of theatre and entertainment.

Theories about the ghosts' origins and motivations

THE THEATRE ROYAL, Drury Lane, located in London's West End, has been a hub of theatrical activity for over 300 years. With such a long and storied history, it's no surprise that the theatre has a reputation for being one of the most haunted in London. Many theories have been put forward to explain the origins and motivations of the ghosts that are said to haunt the theatre.

One theory is that the ghosts are former performers who loved the theatre so much that they never wanted to leave. Some people believe that the ghost of actor Charles Macklin, who died in 1797, still lingers in the theatre, watching over rehearsals and performances. Macklin was famous for his portrayal of Shylock in Shakespeare's "The Merchant of

Venice," and some people believe that his ghost can still be seen sitting in the stalls, watching the stage.

Another theory is that the ghosts are the spirits of theatre-goers who died while attending performances at the theatre. The most famous of these is the ghost of the "Man in Grey." Legend has it that the Man in Grey is the ghost of a man who was murdered in the theatre in the 18th century. His ghost has been seen wandering the theatre, dressed in a grey cloak and tri-cornered hat.

There are also reports of a ghostly woman who is said to haunt the theatre's Royal Box. Some people believe that she is the ghost of a former theatre-goer who was so entranced by a performance that she died of excitement. Others believe that she is the ghost of a former actress who performed at the theatre.

In addition to these well-known ghosts, there have been reports of other supernatural phenomena at the theatre. Some people have reported feeling a cold breeze when walking through the theatre, even when the weather outside is warm. Others have reported hearing strange noises, such as footsteps or the sound of someone whispering.

There have also been reports of objects moving on their own and doors opening and closing by themselves. Some people have reported seeing ghostly apparitions, such as a woman in a white dress or a figure wearing a top hat and tails.

Despite the many theories that have been put forward to explain the hauntings at the Theatre Royal, Drury Lane, no one really knows for sure why the ghosts are there or what they want. Some people believe that the ghosts are simply attached to the theatre and cannot move on to the afterlife, while others believe that they are trying to communicate something to the living.

Regardless of the origins and motivations of the ghosts, one thing is certain: they have become an integral part of the theatre's history and lore. From the Man in Grey to the ghostly woman in the Royal Box, the ghosts of the Theatre Royal, Drury Lane, continue to fascinate and intrigue visitors to this day.

Personal accounts of ghostly experiences

THE THEATRE ROYAL, Drury Lane, located in London's West End, is one of the oldest and most haunted theatres in the world. Opened in 1663, the theatre has a rich history of performances by legendary actors and performers, and has been the site of many ghostly encounters over the years.

One of the most famous ghostly sightings at the Theatre Royal, Drury Lane is that of the "Man in Grey," who is said to haunt the upper circle of the theatre. Legend has it that the man was a nobleman who had an affair with an actress who performed at the theatre in the 18th century. When the actress became pregnant, the nobleman promised to marry her, but instead abandoned her and their child. In despair, the actress threw herself from the upper circle and died on stage. The Man in Grey is said to be the vengeful ghost of the nobleman who now haunts the upper circle of the theatre, seeking redemption for his actions.

Another ghostly encounter at the theatre is that of the "Phantom of the Opera." The story goes that in the early 20th century, a stagehand named Joe was killed in a freak accident while working on the set of a production of the musical "The Phantom of the Opera." Since then, many people have reported seeing a figure dressed in black, wearing a fedora and a long coat, roaming the theatre's backstage areas. Some believe that this is the ghost of Joe, still haunting the theatre where he died.

In addition to these famous ghostly sightings, there have been many other reports of ghostly encounters at the Theatre Royal, Drury Lane. Visitors and staff members have reported hearing strange noises, footsteps, and even whispers in empty rooms. Some have reported feeling cold spots or sudden gusts of wind, even when there is no source for them. Others have reported seeing ghostly apparitions or feeling a presence in the theatre when no one else is around.

There are many theories about the origins and motivations of the ghosts that haunt the Theatre Royal, Drury Lane. Some believe that they are the spirits of former actors or performers who loved the theatre so much that they have never left. Others believe that they are the ghosts of people who died in or around the theatre, and who have remained there in spirit form.

Still, others believe that the ghosts are drawn to the theatre's rich history and energy, and that they simply enjoy being a part of the theatre's legacy. Whatever their origins and motivations may be, there is no denying the fact that the ghosts of the Theatre Royal, Drury Lane have become an integral part of the theatre's history and lore.

Many people who have experienced ghostly encounters at the Theatre Royal, Drury Lane have reported feeling a sense of awe and wonder, as if they have been transported back in time to a bygone era. Others have reported feeling a sense of unease or even fear, as if they are being watched or followed by an unseen presence.

Despite the many ghostly sightings and paranormal experiences that have been reported at the theatre over the years, the staff members and performers at the Theatre Royal, Drury Lane remain committed to keeping the theatre open and accessible to the public. They see the ghosts as a part of the theatre's rich history and legacy, and as a reminder of the many performers who have graced its stage over the centuries.

The Theatre Royal, Drury Lane is a place steeped in history and legend, and its many ghostly sightings and paranormal experiences only add to its mystique and allure. Whether you believe in ghosts or not, there is no denying the fact that the theatre has a certain energy and presence that draws people to it, time and time again.

EDWARD TURNER

Chapter 8: The Spaniards Inn

The history of the Spaniards Inn

The Spaniards Inn is a historic pub located on the edge of Hampstead Heath in London. The inn has a rich history that dates back to the early 16th century, and it has been a popular destination for locals and tourists alike for centuries. The Spaniards Inn has a special place in the history of English literature, as it was frequented by some of the country's most famous writers and artists, including John Keats and William Hogarth.

The origins of the Spaniards Inn can be traced back to the 16th century, when it was known as the "Nag's Head". The inn was popular with travellers who were passing through the area, and it quickly became a popular destination for locals as well. In the late 18th century, the inn was renamed the Spaniards Inn, after a group of Spanish merchants who used to meet there.

The Spaniards Inn has played an important role in English literature for centuries. It was a popular haunt of some of the country's most famous writers and artists, including John Keats, who is said to have written his famous poem "Ode to a Nightingale" while sitting in the inn's garden. The poet Percy Bysshe Shelley was also a regular visitor to the Spaniards Inn, and it is said that he wrote parts of his famous poem "Queen Mab" while sitting in the inn's garden.

The Spaniards Inn has also been featured in several works of fiction over the years. It is mentioned in Charles Dickens' novel "The Pickwick Papers", and it is said to be the inspiration for the inn in Bram Stoker's famous novel "Dracula". In recent years, the inn has continued to attract a diverse range of visitors, including locals, tourists, and literary enthusiasts.

Today, the Spaniards Inn is a popular destination for visitors to London. The pub has retained much of its historic charm, with its original oak beams, open fireplaces, and cosy interior. The inn also features a large outdoor garden, which is a popular spot for visitors to enjoy a drink or a meal on a sunny day.

In addition to its literary connections, the Spaniards Inn is also known for its ghostly sightings and paranormal experiences. Over the years, several visitors and staff members have reported strange occurrences, including the sound of footsteps, disembodied voices, and strange cold spots. Many believe that the inn is haunted by the ghost of a highwayman who was killed on the nearby heath in the 18th century.

Despite its ghostly reputation, the Spaniards Inn remains a popular destination for visitors to London. Whether you are a literary enthusiast, a history buff, or simply looking for a cosy pub with a rich history, the Spaniards Inn is well worth a visit.

The most famous ghostly sightings

THE SPANIARDS INN IS a historic pub located in the Hampstead area of London, England. The pub dates back to the 16th century and is famous for its literary connections, having been visited by famous writers such as Charles Dickens and John Keats. However, the Spaniards Inn is also known for its ghostly sightings and paranormal experiences.

One of the most famous ghostly sightings at the Spaniards Inn is that of a ghostly coach and horses that reportedly appears outside the pub. According to legend, the coach and horses belonged to the infamous highwayman, Dick Turpin, who is said to have frequented the pub during his criminal career. The ghostly coach and horses have been seen by numerous witnesses over the years, with some even claiming to have heard the sound of galloping hooves and the clatter of wheels on the cobbles.

Another ghostly sighting at the Spaniards Inn is that of a woman dressed in a flowing white gown. The woman is said to appear in the upstairs room of the pub, which was once used as a stable. According to legend, the woman was a former landlady of the pub who died in mysterious circumstances. She is said to have been murdered by her husband, who was jealous of her flirting with the pub's customers. Witnesses have reported seeing the ghostly woman walking through the room or standing at the foot of the bed.

One of the more unsettling ghostly experiences reported at the Spaniards Inn is that of a poltergeist that haunts the pub's cellar. The poltergeist is said to be responsible for moving objects around the cellar and making loud banging noises. Some witnesses have even reported feeling a sense of unease or being watched while in the cellar.

There have also been reports of other ghostly sightings and paranormal experiences at the Spaniards Inn. Some witnesses have reported seeing a ghostly figure walking through the pub's courtyard, while others have reported feeling a sudden drop in temperature or feeling a strange presence in the pub's upstairs rooms.

Many theories have been put forward to explain the ghosts and paranormal experiences at the Spaniards Inn. Some believe that the ghostly coach and horses are connected to the pub's past as a coaching inn, while others believe that the woman in the white gown is the ghost of the murdered landlady. The poltergeist in the cellar has been attributed to the pub's former use as a storage space for smugglers and criminals.

Despite the many theories, the true nature of the ghosts and paranormal experiences at the Spaniards Inn remains a mystery. However, the pub's reputation as a haunted location has only added to its appeal and popularity. Visitors to the Spaniards Inn can enjoy a drink in the pub's historic interior while keeping an eye out for any ghostly sightings or experiences.

Theories about the nature of the hauntings

THE SPANIARDS INN IS a historic pub in Hampstead, London, with a reputation for being one of the most haunted pubs in the city. Many people who have visited the pub have reported strange and unexplainable occurrences, leading to theories about the nature of the hauntings and why they persist.

GHOSTS OF LONDON: TEN HAUNTED PLACES IN THE CITY

One of the most popular theories is that the ghosts are linked to the pub's long and eventful history. The pub has been around since the early 17th century and has seen many famous visitors over the years, including Keats, Shelley, and Dickens. Some people believe that the spirits of these famous writers still haunt the pub, either because they were particularly fond of the place in life, or because they have unfinished business.

Another theory is that the pub is haunted by the ghosts of former patrons or staff members. There have been many reports of strange sounds and apparitions, particularly in the upper floors of the building. Some people believe that these ghosts may be connected to the pub's former use as a coaching inn and may be linked to the many people who passed through the building on their travels.

There are also theories that the hauntings may be linked to the nearby Hampstead Heath, which has a reputation for being a place of supernatural activity. Some people believe that the pub's location on the edge of the heath may make it particularly susceptible to paranormal activity, and that the ghosts may be drawn to the building for this reason.

Whatever the cause of the hauntings, there is no doubt that the Spaniards Inn has a reputation for being a particularly spooky place. Visitors have reported strange sensations, including feelings of being watched or touched, as well as unexplained noises and apparitions. Many people have reported seeing the ghost of a former landlord, who is said to have died in the pub, while others have reported the presence of a ghostly dog, which is said to haunt the building and the surrounding area.

Despite the many reports of hauntings, the owners of the Spaniards Inn have always been keen to play down the pub's reputation as a haunted location. However, they have also been careful to preserve the pub's historic character and have made efforts to maintain the building in its original state. Today, visitors to the pub can still see many of the original features, including a large open fireplace and wooden beams, which add to the pub's charm and character.

The Spaniards Inn is a pub with a long and eventful history, which has led to many theories about the nature of its hauntings. Whether the ghosts are the spirits of former patrons or famous writers, or are linked to the nearby Hampstead Heath, there is no doubt that the pub has a reputation for being a particularly spooky place. Visitors who are brave enough to venture inside may well experience some strange and unexplainable occurrences, making it a must-visit location for those interested in the paranormal.

Personal accounts of ghostly experiences

THE SPANIARDS INN IS a historic pub located in Hampstead, London. It dates back to the 16th century and has become well known for its ghostly sightings and paranormal experiences. Many visitors and staff have reported strange occurrences over the years, and some have even claimed to have seen ghosts.

One of the most famous stories involves the ghost of Dick Turpin, an infamous highwayman who is said to have frequented the pub in the 18th century. Turpin was executed in 1739 for his crimes, but some believe that his spirit still haunts the Spaniards Inn. There have been numerous sightings of a ghostly figure dressed in 18th-century clothing, believed to be Turpin himself. Some have reported hearing the sound of horse hooves and the clink of spurs, as if a horse and rider were passing by.

Another ghost that is said to haunt the pub is that of a young girl named Mary. She is believed to have been a regular at the inn in the 19th century and died tragically in a nearby pond. Many visitors have reported seeing her ghostly figure sitting alone in the bar or wandering through the halls.

In addition to these well-known spirits, there have also been reports of other ghostly occurrences at the Spaniards Inn. Some visitors have claimed to feel a sudden chill in the air or to have heard strange noises when no one else is around. Others have reported objects moving on their own or strange smells that can't be explained.

There are many theories about the nature of the hauntings and why they persist at the Spaniards Inn. Some believe that the pub's long and storied history has left an imprint on the building, making it a magnet for paranormal activity. Others speculate that the spirits of those who died tragic or violent deaths in the area may still linger, unable to move on.

Whatever the cause, the ghostly sightings and paranormal experiences at the Spaniards Inn continue to intrigue visitors and staff alike. Many people visit the pub specifically to see if they can spot a ghost, and the pub's reputation as a haunted hotspot has only grown over the years.

Despite the spooky reputation of the Spaniards Inn, it remains a popular destination for locals and tourists alike. The pub's historic charm and literary connections, combined with its ghostly reputation, make it a unique and unforgettable experience for those who visit. Whether you're a believer in the paranormal or simply enjoy a good ghost story, the Spaniards Inn is definitely worth a visit. Who knows, you might just have your own encounter with a ghost!

GHOSTS OF LONDON: TEN HAUNTED PLACES IN THE CITY

Chapter 9: The Savoy Hotel

History of the Savoy Hotel

The Savoy Hotel is one of the most iconic hotels in London, located in the heart of the city on the north bank of the River Thames. The hotel has a rich history that dates back to 1889 when it was opened by Richard D'Oyly Carte, the impresario behind the famous Savoy Theatre. The Savoy Hotel quickly became a favourite among the rich and famous, and over the years, it has played host to countless celebrities, politicians, and royalty.

The Savoy Hotel was designed to be a luxurious and opulent retreat for the elite of society. The hotel was the first in the world to be fitted with electric lights and elevators, and it was the first hotel in Britain to offer en suite bathrooms in every room. The hotel's décor was inspired by the French Renaissance, with sumptuous fabrics, gilded furniture, and lavish chandeliers creating a truly elegant and sophisticated atmosphere.

Over the years, the Savoy Hotel has been a magnet for the rich and famous, and it has played host to many of the world's most iconic figures. The list of famous guests who have stayed at the Savoy Hotel reads like a who's who of the entertainment industry, including Charlie Chaplin, Marilyn Monroe, and Frank Sinatra. The hotel has also hosted many prominent politicians and members of the royal family, including Winston Churchill, Queen Elizabeth II, and Princess Diana.

The Savoy Hotel has played an important role in the social and cultural history of London. The hotel's famous American Bar has long been a popular meeting place for writers, artists, and musicians, and it has been the setting for many literary and artistic works. The hotel was also the location of the first public demonstration of the telephone in Britain when Alexander Graham Bell made the first telephone call from the hotel in 1878.

Despite its glamorous reputation, the Savoy Hotel has had its fair share of setbacks over the years. During the Second World War, the hotel was requisitioned by the government and used as a base for American servicemen. The hotel was badly damaged by bombing during the war, and it was closed for several years before reopening in 1953. In 2007, the hotel was closed for a three-year renovation project, during which time it was extensively refurbished and modernised.

Today, the Savoy Hotel continues to be a popular destination for visitors to London, offering the same level of luxury and sophistication that it has always been known for. The hotel's iconic features, such as the American Bar and the Savoy Grill, continue to attract guests from around the world, and the hotel remains one of the most prestigious addresses in the city.

The Savoy Hotel is a true icon of London's hospitality industry, with a rich history that spans over a century. From its opulent design to its famous guests, the Savoy Hotel has played an important role in the cultural and social history of the city, and it continues to be a favourite among the rich and famous. With its timeless elegance and unparalleled luxury, the Savoy Hotel is a true symbol of London's enduring glamour and sophistication.

The most famous ghostly sightings

THE SAVOY HOTEL, LOCATED in the heart of London, is a luxurious and historic hotel that has hosted many famous guests over the years, including royalty, celebrities, and politicians. However, it is not just the living who have checked into the Savoy; many have reported ghostly sightings and paranormal experiences within its walls. Let's take a look at some of the most famous ghostly sightings and paranormal experiences of the Savoy Hotel.

One of the most famous ghostly sightings at the Savoy Hotel is that of the ghost of Claude Grahame-White, a pioneering British aviator who died in 1959. Guests have reported seeing his ghostly figure walking through the walls of the hotel's Lancaster Ballroom, which was once a part of the Savoy Theatre where Grahame-White's wife, the actress Dorothy Dickson, performed. Some guests have even claimed to have seen Grahame-White sitting in one of the chairs in the ballroom, dressed in his flying gear.

Another famous ghostly sighting at the Savoy Hotel is that of the ghost of a young woman who is said to haunt the fifth floor. According to legend, she was a maid who worked at the hotel and fell in love with a guest. When their relationship was discovered, the guest was ordered to leave the hotel, and the maid was heartbroken. She eventually took her own life by jumping from the fifth-floor balcony. Since then, guests have reported hearing her footsteps and seeing her ghostly figure on the fifth floor.

In addition to these famous sightings, there have been many other reported paranormal experiences at the Savoy Hotel. Some guests have reported feeling a sudden drop in temperature, hearing unexplained noises, and feeling a sense of being watched or followed. Others have reported seeing objects move on their own or feeling a sudden gust of wind in a room with no windows or doors open.

So, what is the nature of these hauntings, and why do they persist? There are several theories about why the Savoy Hotel is haunted. One theory is that the hotel's long and storied history has left an imprint on the building, creating a sort of residual energy that manifests as ghostly sightings and paranormal experiences. Another theory is that the ghosts at the Savoy are the spirits of former guests or employees who are still attached to the hotel for some reason.

Whatever the reason for these hauntings, the Savoy Hotel has embraced its paranormal reputation and even offers ghost tours for guests who are interested in learning more about the hotel's ghostly inhabitants. The hotel staff has also reported their own experiences with the hotel's ghosts, including unexplained noises and objects moving on their own.

The Savoy Hotel is not just a luxurious place to stay; it is also a place with a rich history and many ghostly inhabitants. From the ghost of Claude Grahame-White to the haunted fifth floor, there are many famous ghostly sightings and paranormal experiences at the Savoy Hotel. While the reasons for these hauntings may be unknown, they add to the hotel's charm and mystique, making it a unique and unforgettable destination for visitors to London.

Theories about the ghosts' origins and motivations

THE SAVOY HOTEL, ONE of London's most prestigious hotels, has a long history of paranormal activity. Over the years, many guests and staff members have reported seeing apparitions, hearing strange noises, and feeling an eerie presence in various parts of the hotel. Theories abound about the ghosts' origins and motivations, ranging from tragic historical events to the hotel's luxurious past.

One theory is that the ghosts are connected to the Savoy's long and illustrious history. The hotel was founded in 1889 by Richard D'Oyly Carte, the impresario behind the Savoy Theatre and the Gilbert and Sullivan operettas. The hotel quickly became a favourite of royalty, politicians, and celebrities. Many famous people have stayed at the Savoy, including Winston Churchill, Marilyn Monroe, and Frank Sinatra. Some believe that the ghosts are the spirits of former guests who loved the hotel so much they never wanted to leave.

Another theory is that the ghosts are connected to Savoy's dark past. During World War II, the hotel was used as a base of operations by the American OSS (the predecessor to the CIA) and British intelligence agencies. The hotel's basement was used to store classified documents and was also the site of a secret radio room used to communicate with agents in Nazi-occupied Europe. Some believe that the ghosts are the spirits of spies who died during their missions or were killed by enemy agents.

Yet another theory is that the ghosts are connected to the hotel's many tragedies. Over the years, several guests and staff members have died in the hotel under mysterious circumstances. One famous case involves the death of a maid named Caroline who worked at the hotel in the early 20th century. Caroline was pregnant by one of the hotel's chefs, and when he refused to marry her, she hanged herself in her room. Many guests have reported seeing Caroline's ghost in the corridors and staircases of the hotel.

One of the most famous ghosts at the Savoy is that of a woman in a white dress. The ghost is often seen wandering the halls of the hotel or sitting at the bar of the American Bar. Some believe that the woman is the ghost of a former guest who died in the hotel, while others think she may be the ghost of a young woman who drowned in the nearby Thames River.

There have also been reports of a ghostly figure in a top hat and tails, who is said to be the ghost of Richard D'Oyly Carte himself. Carte died in 1901, but some believe that he still haunts the hotel, keeping an eye on his beloved Savoy.

Regardless of their origins, the ghosts of the Savoy Hotel continue to fascinate and intrigue visitors and staff alike. The hotel even offers ghost tours for guests who want to learn more about its haunted history. Whether they are remnants of the hotel's glorious past, the spirits of those who died tragically, or simply figments of the imagination, the ghosts of the Savoy are an integral part of the hotel's unique charm and character.

Personal accounts of ghostly experiences

THE SAVOY HOTEL IN London has been known for its elegance and luxurious accommodations since it first opened its doors in 1889. However, over the years, it has also gained a reputation for being one of the most haunted places in London. With its rich history and long list of famous guests, it's no surprise that many people have reported paranormal experiences during their stay.

One of the most commonly reported ghostly sightings is that of a man dressed in black who is often seen in the hotel's public areas, including the lobby and restaurants. This figure is believed to be the ghost of Richard D'Oyly Carte, the original owner of the hotel. He is said to appear to guests and staff members alike, sometimes making his presence known by moving objects or turning lights on and off. Some people have even reported feeling a sudden drop in temperature when he is near.

Another ghostly presence that has been reported at the Savoy is that of a woman in a long white dress. She is believed to be the spirit of an actress who took her own life in one of the hotel's rooms after being jilted by her lover. She has been spotted wandering the halls of the hotel, and some guests have even claimed to see her reflection in mirrors. Others have reported feeling a sense of sadness or despair when they encounter her.

The third most commonly reported ghostly presence at the Savoy is that of a small boy who is said to roam the halls of the fifth floor. It is unclear who this boy might be, but some theories suggest that he may have been a victim of one of the hotel's fires, which occurred in 1904 and 1916. Guests who have encountered the boy have reported feeling a sense of unease or fear, as if he is trying to communicate something to them.

In addition to these three main ghosts, there have been reports of other paranormal activity at the Savoy Hotel. Some guests have reported hearing disembodied voices or footsteps, while others have reported seeing objects move on their own. Some have even claimed to feel a physical presence pressing down on them as they slept, as if someone or something was trying to suffocate them.

There are many theories about why these ghosts continue to haunt the Savoy Hotel. Some believe that they are simply residual energy left behind from traumatic events that occurred in the building's past, while others believe that they are the actual spirits of people who died there. Some people even believe that the hotel's luxurious atmosphere and high level of energy draw in paranormal entities from other dimensions.

Whatever the reason may be, it's clear that the Savoy Hotel has a long history of paranormal activity. Many guests who have stayed there have reported eerie experiences that they can't explain. Whether you're a believer in the paranormal or not, there's no denying that the Savoy Hotel is a fascinating place with a rich history and many intriguing stories to tell. If you ever have the chance to stay there, keep your eyes and ears open - you never know what you might encounter.

Chapter 10: The Old Bailey

The history of the Old Bailey

The Old Bailey, also known as the Central Criminal Court, is one of the most significant buildings in the United Kingdom's legal history. Located in the heart of London, this iconic building has played a vital role in the administration of justice for over 400 years.

The history of the Old Bailey dates back to the 16th century when a courthouse was built on the site in 1539. However, it was not until the 17th century that the building became known as the Old Bailey. The name is believed to have been derived from the nearby street of the same name, which was named after the Old Bailey's original owner, Sir William de Bailleul.

In 1674, the courthouse was rebuilt to accommodate the growing number of legal cases being heard in London. This new building included a central hall where trials could be conducted, as well as various other rooms for the use of judges and lawyers. Over the years, the Old Bailey has undergone several renovations and extensions, but it has always remained an integral part of the city's legal landscape.

Throughout its history, the Old Bailey has been associated with some of the most significant trials in English legal history. It has been the site of many high-profile cases, including those of Jack the Ripper, Dr. Crippen, and the Kray twins. The courtroom has also seen the trial and conviction of numerous political figures, including William Wallace, Guy Fawkes, and even Anne Boleyn, the second wife of Henry VIII.

The Old Bailey has also been the setting for several significant legal reforms. In 1736, the Gaols Act established the right of prisoners to a speedy trial, while the 1836 Prison Act led to the construction of new prisons throughout England and Wales. The 1879 Criminal Law Amendment Act introduced a series of sweeping reforms to the legal system, including the abolition of public executions.

Despite its rich history, the Old Bailey is perhaps best known for its role in the modern justice system. Today, the courthouse is the venue for many criminal trials, including those of terrorist suspects and high-profile cases such as the 2006 liquid bomb plot. The building's courtroom, with its dock for the accused, bench for the judge, and jury box, remains an iconic symbol of the English legal system.

In addition to its legal significance, the Old Bailey is also a popular tourist destination. Visitors can take guided tours of the courthouse, where they can learn about its history and view its many historic features. These include the dock where many infamous criminals have stood trial, the judges' chambers, and the holding cells where prisoners were once held before being brought to court.

The Old Bailey's history has also been the subject of many books, films, and television shows. Its iconic status has made it a popular location for filmmakers and has been featured in movies such as Oliver Twist, The Mummy Returns, and Bridget Jones's Diary.

The Old Bailey is an iconic and historic building that has played a significant role in the development of the English legal system. Its courtroom has seen some of the most famous criminal trials in history, and its legal reforms have had a profound impact on the administration of justice in England and Wales. The building's rich history, combined with its modern-day role as a courthouse and popular tourist destination, make it a must-see location for anyone interested in the legal history of the United Kingdom.

The most famous ghostly sightings

THE OLD BAILEY, ALSO known as the Central Criminal Court of England and Wales, is one of the most famous and historic courts in the world. With its rich history dating back over 400 years, it is no surprise that many tales of hauntings and paranormal activity have been associated with this iconic institution. Let's explore some of the most famous ghostly sightings and paranormal experiences of the Old Bailey.

One of the most commonly reported sightings is that of a mysterious woman dressed in black. She is said to appear on the stairs leading to the courtrooms and is believed to be the ghost of a woman who was once sentenced to death in the Old Bailey. Some believe she may have been wrongly accused and executed, hence her ghostly presence in the building.

Another ghostly sighting is that of a young girl who is often seen wandering the halls of the Old Bailey. Her appearance is said to be that of a Victorian era child, and some believe she may have been a victim of one of the many trials that took place at the court during that time period.

The ghost of a former judge, known as "the Hanging Judge" also reportedly haunts the Old Bailey. Judge Jeffreys was known for his harsh sentencing and was responsible for the execution of many prisoners during his tenure. Some say his ghost still roams the halls of the Old Bailey seeking out those who he believes are guilty of crimes.

Another famous sighting is that of the ghostly figure of a man in a top hat and cape, who is often seen pacing back and forth in the cells of the Old Bailey. It is said that he was a former prisoner who was held in the cells before his execution, and his ghostly presence can still be felt in the building.

Some also report hearing strange noises, such as whispers and footsteps, in the courtrooms and halls of the Old Bailey. These unexplained sounds are often attributed to the ghosts of former prisoners and judges who still haunt the building.

While there are many theories as to why the Old Bailey is haunted, one of the most popular is that the building's dark and violent history has left an imprint on the structure. With so many executions, trials, and hangings having taken place within its walls over the centuries, it is believed that the energy of these events has somehow become trapped within the building, leading to the numerous ghostly sightings and paranormal experiences reported by visitors and staff.

Despite its haunted reputation, the Old Bailey remains an important symbol of justice and the rule of law in England and Wales. It continues to serve as a vital institution for the administration of justice, and its historic significance is recognized around the world.

The Old Bailey's long and storied history has left an indelible mark on the building, with many tales of hauntings and paranormal activity being associated with this iconic institution. While some may dismiss these stories as mere superstition, others firmly believe in the existence of ghosts and spirits within the building. Whether or not these sightings are real, they serve as a testament to the Old Bailey's enduring legacy as one of the most important legal institutions in the world.

Theories about the ghosts' origins and motivations

THE OLD BAILEY, ALSO known as the Central Criminal Court of England and Wales, is one of the most well-known and historic buildings in London. The building has been the site of countless criminal trials throughout its history, and it is no surprise that it has also been the site of many alleged paranormal experiences.

One theory about the ghosts of the Old Bailey is that they are the spirits of those who were executed at the site. The Old

Bailey was the site of numerous public executions until the mid-19th century, and it is believed that some of the executed individuals still haunt the building. There have been reports of ghostly apparitions of men and women in period clothing, as well as disembodied voices and footsteps.

Another theory is that the building's long history of criminal trials has created an atmosphere that is conducive to paranormal activity. The intense emotions that are often present in a criminal trial, such as fear, anger, and sadness, may leave an imprint on the building's energy, resulting in ghostly activity. Some visitors to the Old Bailey have reported feeling a sense of unease or foreboding in certain areas of the building.

A more specific theory about the ghosts of the Old Bailey relates to the infamous case of the Ratcliffe Highway murders. In 1811, a series of brutal murders took place on Ratcliffe Highway, and the investigation and trial became a sensation. One of the suspects, John Williams, committed suicide in his cell at the Old Bailey before he could be brought to trial. Some people believe that Williams' spirit still haunts the building, and there have been reports of a ghostly figure wearing a long coat and top hat in the area where Williams' cell used to be.

Finally, some paranormal investigators believe that the Old Bailey may be a site of residual haunting. This theory posits that certain traumatic or emotional events can leave an imprint on a location, resulting in repeated ghostly activity. In the case of the Old Bailey, the building has been the site of countless criminal trials, many of which involved intense emotions and high stakes. It is possible that this history has left an imprint on the building, resulting in the paranormal activity that some visitors and staff have reported.

The Old Bailey is a building with a long and storied history, and it is no surprise that it has become a site of paranormal interest. The theories about the ghosts' origins and motivations of the Old Bailey are varied and complex, reflecting the building's rich history and the many different events and people that have passed through its halls. Whether or not the Old Bailey is truly haunted is a matter of personal belief, but the stories and legends surrounding the building are sure to continue to captivate and intrigue visitors for years to come.

Personal accounts of ghostly experiences

THE OLD BAILEY, ALSO known as the Central Criminal Court, is one of the most famous courtrooms in the world. With a history that dates back to the 16th century, it has witnessed some of the most notorious trials in British history. However, it's not just the trials that have made the Old Bailey famous - it's also the ghost stories that surround the building.

Many people believe that the Old Bailey is haunted by the ghosts of those who have been tried and executed within its walls. There have been numerous reports of strange noises, footsteps, and apparitions throughout the building. Here are some of the most famous ghostly sightings and paranormal experiences of the Old Bailey.

One of the most famous ghostly sightings is that of the ghost of William Calcraft, a notorious hangman who carried out executions at the Old Bailey in the mid-19th century. According to legend, his ghost can still be seen in the courtroom where he used to perform his grim duties. He is said to appear as a tall, gaunt figure dressed in black, and is often accompanied by the sound of creaking rope.

Another famous ghostly sighting is that of the ghost of Sarah Malcolm, who was tried and executed for murder in 1733. Her ghost is said to haunt the staircase that leads to the cells beneath the Old Bailey. Witnesses have reported seeing a woman in a long dress walking up the stairs, only to disappear into thin air.

The cells beneath the Old Bailey are also said to be haunted, with many people reporting strange noises and ghostly apparitions. Some have even reported feeling a cold hand touching them as they walk through the cells.

One particularly chilling story involves the ghost of a man who was hanged for murder in the 18th century. According to legend, his ghost would appear to people in the cells and ask them for a drink of water. Those who refused were said to be cursed, while those who gave him water would find themselves haunted by his ghost for the rest of their lives.

Theories about the origins and motivations of the ghosts at the Old Bailey vary. Some believe that the spirits of those who were executed there are trapped in the building, unable to move on to the afterlife. Others believe that the ghosts are simply residual energy left behind by the traumatic events that have taken place there over the centuries.

GHOSTS OF LONDON: TEN HAUNTED PLACES IN THE CITY

Whatever the reason for the hauntings, there is no denying that the Old Bailey has a rich and fascinating history. From the infamous trials of Jack the Ripper and Dr. Crippen to the ghostly sightings and paranormal experiences, the Old Bailey remains one of the most intriguing and mysterious buildings in London. Whether you believe in ghosts or not, a visit to the Old Bailey is sure to send shivers down your spine.

EDWARD TURNER

Conclusion

Throughout this book, we have explored some of the most haunted places in London, delving into their histories, famous ghostly sightings, theories about their origins and motivations, and personal accounts of ghostly experiences.

We began by exploring the Tower of London, one of the most famous landmarks in London, which has a long and bloody history. The ghosts of Anne Boleyn, Lady Jane Grey, and the Princes in the Tower are said to haunt the Tower, along with other ghostly figures. Theories about their origins range from residual hauntings to restless spirits seeking justice.

We then turned to the Grenadier Pub, which has a reputation as one of the most haunted pubs in London. Theories about the ghosts include soldiers who were punished for breaking military laws, as well as the ghost of a young woman who died tragically. Personal accounts of ghostly experiences include glasses moving on their own and a ghostly presence in the upstairs room.

The Bank of England also has a long and fascinating history, and is said to be haunted by several ghosts, including the ghost of Sarah Whitehead. Theories about the ghosts range from restless spirits seeking revenge to residual hauntings. Personal accounts include the feeling of being watched and unexplained cold spots.

The Theatre Royal, Drury Lane, is another haunted location with a rich history and several ghostly sightings. Theories about the ghosts include the ghost of a man who was murdered in the theatre, as well as the ghosts of several famous actors. Personal accounts of ghostly experiences include the sound of footsteps and unexplained shadows.

The Spaniards Inn is a pub with literary connections, as it was a favourite haunt of Charles Dickens and Bram Stoker. It is said to be haunted by several ghosts, including the ghost of Dick Turpin. Theories about the ghosts range from residual hauntings to restless spirits seeking justice. Personal accounts include unexplained footsteps and the feeling of being touched.

The Savoy Hotel, known for its luxury and elegance, is also said to be haunted by several ghosts, including the ghost of Richard D'Oyly Carte. Theories about the ghosts range from residual hauntings to restless spirits seeking revenge. Personal accounts include the feeling of being watched and unexplained noises.

The Old Bailey, the central criminal court in England, is also said to be haunted by several ghosts, including the ghost of a woman who was falsely accused of murder. Theories about the ghosts include residual hauntings as well as restless spirits seeking justice. Personal accounts include the feeling of being watched and unexplained sensations.

Overall, London is a city steeped in history and legend, and its haunted places provide a fascinating insight into its past. Theories about the ghosts range from residual hauntings to restless spirits seeking justice or revenge. Personal accounts of ghostly experiences vary from unexplained noises and cold spots to the feeling of being touched or watched.

While some may dismiss these stories as mere folklore, others believe that they provide evidence of an unseen world beyond our understanding. Whatever your beliefs, the haunted places of London continue to captivate and intrigue us, inviting us to explore their mysteries and uncover the secrets of the past.

London is a city steeped in history, with a rich and often dark past, which has contributed to its reputation as one of the most haunted cities in the world. From the Tower of London to the haunted pubs and hotels scattered throughout the city, London has no shortage of eerie locations and ghostly tales.

One of the reasons why London is considered to be one of the most haunted cities in the world is its extensive history. London has been inhabited for over 2000 years, and in that time, it has seen its fair share of war, plague, and tragedy. Many of the buildings that stand in London today have been around for centuries, and it is believed that the ghosts of the past continue to haunt them.

Another reason why London is considered to be a hotspot for paranormal activity is the sheer number of people who have lived and died there over the centuries. With a population of over 8 million people, London is one of the largest and most densely populated cities in the world. It is estimated that over 200,000 people are buried in the city's graveyards, many of which have been built over or built upon, leading to reports of ghostly sightings and strange occurrences.

Furthermore, London's cultural and literary legacy has also contributed to its reputation as a city of ghosts. From the works of Charles Dickens to the plays of William Shakespeare, London's rich literary history has often centred on the supernatural and the macabre. Many of the most famous ghost stories and legends of London have been immortalised in literature, from the ghost of Anne Boleyn haunting the Tower of London to the legend of Sweeney Todd, the Demon Barber of Fleet Street.

In addition to its history, population, and literary legacy, London's architecture also plays a role in its reputation as a haunted city. The city is home to a vast array of buildings, from ancient castles to modern skyscrapers, and each has its own unique history and legends. Many of these buildings are said to be haunted by the ghosts of those who once lived or worked there, and the stories and legends associated with them have been passed down through the generations.

Finally, London's status as a global capital and tourist destination has also contributed to its reputation as a city of ghosts. Visitors from all over the world come to London to explore its history, culture, and architecture, and many are drawn to the city's haunted locations. This has led to a thriving ghost tourism industry in London, with ghost walks, ghost hunts, and other paranormal-themed activities available for those who want to experience the city's spooky side for themselves.

GHOSTS OF LONDON: TEN HAUNTED PLACES IN THE CITY

London's extensive history, large population, cultural and literary legacy, architecture, and tourism industry all contribute to its reputation as one of the most haunted cities in the world. The city's many haunted locations, from the Tower of London to the haunted pubs and hotels, continue to fascinate and terrify visitors and locals alike, and the stories and legends associated with them show no signs of disappearing any time soon. Whether you believe in ghosts or not, London's reputation as a city of ghosts is here to stay.

As we come to the end of this book exploring the haunted history of London, I want to take a moment to express my gratitude to you. Thank you for joining me on this journey as we delved into some of the city's most intriguing and spine-tingling tales of the paranormal.

From the Tower of London to the Old Bailey, from the Theatre Royal, Drury Lane to the Savoy Hotel, we have explored some of London's most famous and haunted locations. We have heard stories of ghostly apparitions, unexplained noises, and inexplicable phenomena that continue to intrigue and fascinate visitors and locals alike.

But why is London considered one of the most haunted cities in the world? There are many possible reasons. One theory is that the city's long and complex history has left behind a residual energy that continues to manifest itself in supernatural ways. Another theory is that the sheer number of people who have lived and died in the city over the centuries has created a kind of psychic residue that lingers on, long after their physical bodies have departed.

Whatever the reason, one thing is certain: London is a city that has captured the imagination of writers, artists, and filmmakers for centuries. It's dark and mysterious corners have inspired countless tales of horror, suspense, and intrigue, and continue to draw visitors from all over the world.

As we close the pages of this book, I hope that you have found it both entertaining and informative. Perhaps you have even been inspired to visit some of the places we have discussed and experience the haunted history of London for yourself. And who knows? Maybe you'll have a ghostly encounter of your own to share someday.

Thank you again for joining me on this journey, and I wish you all the best in your future explorations of the haunted and mysterious corners of our world.

Happy haunting!

Don't miss out!

Visit the website below and you can sign up to receive emails whenever Edward Turner publishes a new book. There's no charge and no obligation.

https://books2read.com/r/B-A-SYIZ-ZRKLC

BOOKS 2 READ

Connecting independent readers to independent writers.

Also by Edward Turner

Ghosts of Paris: Ten Haunted Places in the City of Love
Ghosts of London: Ten Haunted Places in The City

About the Author

Edward Turner is a renowned author who specializes in exploring the realms of ghosts, the paranormal, and cryptids. With a captivating writing style and an insatiable curiosity for the unknown, Turner has garnered a dedicated following of readers who are captivated by his thrilling and eerie tales.

Born with an innate fascination for the supernatural, Turner has spent decades delving into the depths of paranormal phenomena, unearthing captivating stories and untangling mysteries that lie beyond the veil of the ordinary. His extensive research and meticulous attention to detail have earned him a reputation as a leading authority in the field.

Through his books, Turner expertly weaves together chilling accounts of encounters with ghosts, offering readers a glimpse into the ethereal world that coexists alongside our own. His ability to paint vivid portraits of spectral apparitions and convey the haunting atmosphere of haunted locations has made his works both spine-tingling and thought-provoking.

Turner's exploration of the paranormal doesn't stop at ghosts. He also dives into the fascinating world of cryptids—creatures that defy conventional explanation. His in-depth investigations into legendary creatures such as Bigfoot, the Loch Ness Monster, and the Chupacabra showcase his commitment to shedding light on these enigmatic beings.

With each page, Edward Turner's readers are drawn deeper into the enigmatic and unknown. His unique storytelling ability combined with his meticulous research has made him a sought-after author for those with an insatiable thirst for the supernatural. Whether delving into ghostly encounters or unraveling the mysteries of elusive cryptids, Turner's books offer a spine-chilling and immersive reading experience that leaves readers questioning the boundaries of our reality.

Edward Turner's works have earned critical acclaim and numerous accolades within the paranormal genre. He continues to explore the unexplained, captivating readers with his distinctive narrative style and unwavering dedication to unveiling the mysteries that lie hidden in the shadows.